FROM THE OTHER END OF THE WORLD

In memory of my parents, Arthur William Dean (Dixie)
and Dorothy Geraldine Dean (nee Horne).

Dedicated to their granddaughter,
my daughter Vanessa Geraldine Goodman.

From the Other End of the World

"… and a thousand new arrivals from the other end of the world looked at the shore … and wondered what was in store for them."

EDITED BY R. K. DEAN

Edited by R. K. Dean

First published in 2010 by GWW Services
Email: gwwindustries@yahoo.co.uk
Website: www.gwwservices.com
C/o Print House Ltd. PO Box 5544, Hamilton 3242, New Zealand

ISBN 978-0-473-16381-5

Design by Richard Stowers

Printed in Korea through Print House Ltd, Hamilton

Contents

Acknowledgements

This book contains a mixture of original documents and memoirs of various people who immigrated to New Zealand from Great Britain – and never returned. Taken altogether they provide fascinating snapshots of experiences that would have been shared by many other immigrants.

The information in this book is not in any way statistically representative of the experiences of people who came from Great Britain to New Zealand. Firstly, the sample size is far too small. Secondly, as all of these people remained in New Zealand the majority were presumably content with the outcome of their decision to immigrate. The experiences of those who chose to return would make an interesting book of their own. Finally, due to the time that has elapsed since these people sailed, there is a bias towards the experiences of younger immigrants.

My grateful thanks go to Rural Women New Zealand and The New Zealand Society of Genealogists for enabling me to make initial contact with many of the contributors in this book. Special thanks to Phyllis Young for making her late husband's photograph album available. Thanks are also due to Richard Stowers and Jennifer Smith for advice and for their design and editorial skills, and Wellington City Archives – Knowledge Solutions, for their assistance with research. Special thanks also to Sue Hall, and my husband and daughter Stephen and Vanessa Goodman, without whose help and support this book would never have been published.

Finally, the book is only as good as its contributors whom I unreservedly thank for answering my questions and sharing their memories, documents and photographs.

Foreword

As a New Zealander, with a rather sketchy knowledge of how our ancestors came to New Zealand, I was delighted to be asked to "read through" these stories.

Having no idea of what a "£10 Pom" was, I have been fascinated to read the experiences of the immigrants from the UK who left behind all that was familiar for a journey to "The Other End of the World".

These writings capture the very essence of lives which were removed from 'home'.

Most writers thought they would try this adventure and return after the obligatory two years, but as one follows their stories it is interesting to read that the majority have been content to remain here, some not even going 'home' for a visit.

In a time when younger people are not aware of their history for various reasons, stories such as these are so important. If not recorded they will be lost to future generations. This is a valuable record of travel, incidents and early settlement made in this country. There are facts and figures which highlight the differences to today's world.

These narratives portray a common link through the journey by sea but each story is different. Details of shipboard romance, interesting sights, new experiences, expectations unfulfilled. There is fun and laughter but there is sadness too – and in one case, the profoundly moving.

Congratulations to Rachael on bringing together a valuable and interesting collection which provides an insight into an important part of the New Zealand heritage.

Sue Hall

A second-generation New Zealander with 20 years in the education field, now even busier with farming and volunteer work, Sue Hall has always found time to pursue her strong interest in history, especially social history.

CHAPTER 1

Olive Wilkinson

Name	Olive K Wilkinson
Ship	*Rangitiki*
Departure date	May 1946
Arrival date	27 July 1946
Destination	North Island
Marital status	Married a New Zealand Airman (war bride)
Profession	Clerk for Carter Transport in the UK (work of national importance in war time), farmer's wife in New Zealand
Intention	To remain in New Zealand

During the war I was employed as a ledger clerk for a transport company, Carter Paterson and Co Ltd, in the City of London. I was not allowed to join any women's forces (much to my disappointment) as transport was work of national importance. I was also a volunteer for 3½ years at the New Zealand Forces Club in Charing Cross Road, London. Most of what I learnt about New Zealand before meeting my husband was from the servicemen that came to the club. My parents also helped servicemen who had no contacts in the UK. Many were only too happy to talk about their hometowns in New Zealand.

I met my husband on VE Day 1945 and we were married on 5 January 1946. In May 1946 I sailed on the *Rangitiki* from the Tilbury docks, London, England for Wellington, New Zealand. There were about 400 war brides on the ship, some of whom were pregnant and some with one or two children – these brides had not been allowed to travel while the war was on. There were about 200 civilians and a small number of servicemen and their families but they were not allowed to have cabins for themselves.

As I was now married to a New Zealand airman who was returning home, my plans were to remain in New Zealand. We were a close family, though, and I found it very hard to leave them behind, especially as my father had only just passed away, leaving my mother a widow and my brother still only eight.

On the trip out we had a service stop in the Azores (Curacao) where we took bananas back to the ship. The young ones on board had never seen a banana and tried to eat them with the skin still on! We then went through the Panama Canal and had a day visit in Balboa. Carrying on to New Zealand, the ship developed engine trouble and had to return to Panama City, where we remained for 13 days. The American-based communications personnel were very kind during our time there. As we only had salt water to wash with, the American families opened up their homes to the mothers on board so they could use their facilities. Other brides were invited out to various functions during this time, and I was lucky enough to experience a drive along the Canal.

In 1955 we moved onto our farm, a 360 acre returned serviceman settlement farm at Whakamaru. Ours was the first sheep farm at Whakamaru. When we arrived, our farm was at the end of a metal [gravel] road which was very winding and narrow. We had an army camp for neighbours. I recall freezing temperatures, thick fog and being isolated. We had very few amenities – no phone, no power, no water, no mail, no school or bus [Olive had two children by this time]. There were no birds, no worms, and no trees for the first sheep farmers in the area. Our property had just a circle fence – no divided paddocks, and a part-house (650sq feet) with an outside long drop. The first settlers had implement sheds for a house, the part-house came later. Stock and station agents brought our papers and farm requirements from Tokoroa, and the vet also came from Tokoroa. Mangakino was a hydro township and did not cater for farming needs in those days. Groceries were delivered late at night from Buckley's store on Sandal Road.

The very first thing I had to do was learn to cook, since my mother could not risk our precious rations (one egg, 20 ounces butter and one ounce of sugar per person per week), for me to learn during the war.

Grader on a narrow metal [gravel] road in New Zealand.

Photo courtesy of Phyllis Young

I was invited to morning tea many times – scones, jam and cream. Six weeks after my arrival my husband advised that shearers were coming, and I had to cook all those traditional scones for morning and afternoon teas and a huge mutton roast for the shearing gang. For scones, I read the recipe on the Edmonds Baking Powder tin: rub in butter etc, roll out. I had seen my mother making pastry so I rolled out the dough three times then I thought about those rough edges. So I cut them out with a glass, they went into the oven – and came out the same size – my claim to fame for the first "flying saucers".

Later, I phoned my war bride friend at Papakura and asked her how she was getting on, as she was the same as me, no cook. She related a conversation on her husband's arrival home one night, "Smells lovely, roast chicken – did you do a nice stuffing?" "Oh no", said my friend, "no need, it was already stuffed" (the giblets being still inside).

Rationing in England was worse after the war, so I did not have complaints about the food situation in New Zealand. Being on a sheep farm we had meat, milk, butter, cream and plenty of home-grown vegetables. I did miss live theatre shows, though. My friends and I in London used to go every Saturday afternoon (for 2/6 "up in the Gods") to all the theatres in the West-End.

That newly grassed land grew clover prolifically, much to the cost of the first dairy farmers. There are photos of up to 30 cows piled up having died from bloat in one day. These first dairy farms should have been sheep blocks, but to escalate the settlement of returned servicemen, dairy farms were formed throughout the pumice areas of Reporora, Tirohanga, Mihi and Whakamaru.

A dilapidated building was the first Settlers Hall, hot-dog stove for heating and long drop toilets (with plenty of rats). I had taught my two young children by correspondence at first, but as the numbers of farms settled on increased, a school bus came out to take children the 15 miles into Mangakino. It was a long day for the children. In 1960 a new school was built behind Whakamaru Hydro village, and with the expansion of settlements up to Marotiri Junction, another school (Marotiri School) was built in 1961, which my children went to. Then a new hall was built on the hill above the old Whakamaru Settlers' Hall. Women's Division of Federated Farmers (WDFF) [now Rural Women New Zealand] was the only women's group in the area and the Whakamaru Branch had the largest membership in the North Island for a few years. At the time of the opening of the new hall, it was like a Melbourne Cup Day – several members of the WDFF had been taking hat-making classes and all these ladies were wearing their own creations.

Our main social events were centred on the schools, calf clubs, fat-lamb days, end-of-year functions for pupils and parents, and welcoming dances for new settlers to the district.

Our head teacher at Marotiri School was music-orientated, so the school had a good music group. Older pupils were taught ballroom dancing and in their last term before leaving for high school, they invited the school committee and PTA

Photo courtesy of Phyllis Young

Pet calves ready for calf club.

[Parent Teacher Association] Committee members to their dance at the hall. They were not allowed to dance with each other; boys asked the ladies and girls the men, escorting them onto the floor and then back to their seats after the dance. Marotiri School was fortunate to have a very active and dedicated school committee and PTA and within two years we had a swimming pool. Money was earned from the sale of cattle beasts and sheep donated by parents. The library and many other facilities were achieved by the PTA. Ladies also provided tea and sandwiches at sale yards. The school could not get anyone to take on the job of school cleaner so parents went on to a roster; mothers to clean the school, and fathers to look after the school grounds.

For several years the annual Christmas picnic was held on a farmer's property alongside the Waikato River towards Atiamuri. It was known as Dunham's Park. Children's fancy-dress competitions and joint social events during the year helped to keep settlers in touch with each other. As the number of sheep farms increased, a shearing shed was built. That became the venue for our New Year celebrations – "men a bottle of beer and ladies a plate". The children played under the shearing shed while the parents celebrated and danced in the shed. Lots of fun was had by children and adults alike.

In those early days violent electrical storms were experienced and icy cold rain came straight off the Ruapehu and Ngauruhoe mountains – there was no shelter as there were no trees. Water froze in toilet pans, and power lines had frost as thick as your wrist causing failure in power and telephone. With 11 sharing a party line [for the telephone] this made things very difficult. One rainstorm on New Years Eve, covering only a two-mile span, dropped seven inches of rain in an hour. This washed out the S-bend on Tihoi Road, causing farmers from the bottom of the road to come up to see where all the water was coming from. In another storm the week before Christmas, lightning struck a telephone line to a house on Kahu road. Because this cable ran down through the linen cupboard, all the sheets and towels were scorched. Another lightning storm cut through a newly finished fence line alongside an air-strip; and a power pole acting as a conductor welded a teapot to a steel bench (through a window) in a contractor's house on Tihoi Road.

Ragwort was another plague of the district, and until we had our own air-strip [which would enable aerial spraying], the whole family were pulling it out by hand. Even when we did get the go-ahead to spray the ragwort (State Advances helping with the cost), very thick fog hampered the early morning flying so we had to play the waiting game for days on end, getting up at 3.30am to look out at the weather. In those early days hay-making was also a hit-and-miss affair.

An enduring memory, also a highlight for children on the school bus, was the hunt for escaped prisoner, George Wilder [George Wilder, probably New Zealand's most notorious prison escaper, escaped from prison three times]. The children found it very exciting when the school bus was stopped and the police got on board and looked under the seats.

Nowadays this pumice land has farms all the way to Kuratau. Dairy farms have amalgamated and become sheep farms, and sheep farms have amalgamated and become extra large dairy farms. Taupo is only 20 minutes away, and Mangakino has only a small population. The trees are many, the fog is much less and the climate a little warmer.

On the trip out to New Zealand I shared a cabin with five other war brides, one of whom was pregnant with twins. I keep in touch with them all, although only one is now still alive – now 87 years old [as at 2008]. We all went back for visits over the years – I have been home 10 times – but we always came back to New Zealand. My mother and brother came out to New Zealand in 1955, but they could not settle and went back to the UK in 1958.

My husband and I had five children, three daughters and two sons. My two sons both married American women and live in the United States. Two of my daughters are in New Zealand and one in Australia. I have nine grandchildren and one great grandchild. I had a wonderful marriage, although it was sadly cut short when my husband passed away with cancer in 1975. I then moved off the farm, purchased a home with the help of a State Advances Loan, and moved to Tokoroa. In the 1970s women had no input re loans, banks, lay-bys etc. and as all our farming business was conducted through the banks, it was easier to purchase a home than have to worry about establishing a credit rating for banks. A loving family has helped me enjoy my continuing life.

So – I went from being a London-born ledger clerk to a sheep farmer's wife who could not cook! WDFF became my saviour and I have enjoyed all WDFF events. I am still president of the Tokoroa branch. It is a small branch but it keeps me interested. New Zealand is my place to live but Home is still the UK.

Olive joined the Tokoroa Branch of Women's Division of Federated Farmers (WDFF – now Rural Women New Zealand) in 1956. She has held Executive roles at Branch and Provincial level and has been awarded Life Membership to Branch and Provincial. Olive also served her community in many other roles, from starting a play group in 1966 and 23 years as Treasurer of the Women's section of the RSA, to providing care and support for elderly people in Tokoroa. Olive was awarded the Queen's Service Medal in 1993 for her years of service with WDFF.

CHAPTER 2

Eleanor Devine

Name	Eleanor Devine
Ship	SS *Atlantis*
Departure date	29 July 1949
Arrival date	12 September 1949
Destination	North Island
Marital status	Single
Profession	Office worker, qualified shorthand typist
Intention	To remain in New Zealand

My grandfather, Michael Devine, was a seaman in the Merchant Service and he had three sons, Michael the oldest, Brian Arthur and Terry. Brian was my father. At the age of 14 he worked in an office at the East India Docks in London. He must have yearned to sail in one of the big ships, because on hearing one of them was sailing to New Zealand, he rushed home after work to tell his mother they needed a cabin boy. After a lot of persuading and assuring his mother the ship would be returning, he managed to convince her to let him go.

As it happened, the ship didn't return for two years and my father was stranded, so to speak, in New Zealand. In one of the ports he had all his possessions stolen via the porthole and literally was left with only the clothes that he stood up in.

My brother Brian and I never failed to enjoy hearing the various things that happened to my father, who was full of praise for the New Zealand people and always said he would return again one day. On one occasion he was having a bun and drink in a tea-room with a man, presumably from the ship, and unbeknown to each other, neither of them had any money. When they had finished eating, the man told my father to get out as fast as he could and not to stop running and he would pay by doing some dishes or suchlike. My father said he ran for his life! He told us that he got a job as a bellboy at a Wellington hotel and was quite happy there for the rest of his stay, and well looked after.

Our family, Mother, Father, two brothers and I, had just come through a long horrendous war living in Bexley, Kent – known as "Bomb Alley". When my father suggested coming to New Zealand to live, my brother Brian and I were over the moon. The idea was that I would go first as a single assisted immigrant to do office work, and although my family would have had to wait two years for a

Eleanor at Tauranga, New
Zealand. 1950-51.

passage, I could pave the way for them. I had a cousin, Jean, who had married
a New Zealand soldier, Stephen Baker, and lived in George's Drive, Napier, and
I could stay with them. With this plan in mind, I was to make enquiries from
New Zealand House in the Haymarket, which I promptly did. After I'd given my
father all the details he slept on it, and the next day said he had changed his mind.
Brian and I were utterly shattered. We were not too pleased with my father and
told him so.

Cousins are very useful, as another one, Marie, had married an American who
worked in the James Cook Shipping Office in London. He came home one day
to say that he could get a berth for five people on the *Dominion Monarch* if they
could leave in six weeks time. There were now six in our family (my little sister
Linda was born after the war), so with great reluctance they had to leave me
behind.

I was to stay with my aunt and uncle who lived next door to us, and wait for an
assisted passage. I worked in Hatton Gardens, London for the Western Glass
Company; still feeling sad that my family had gone, but also having the comfort

of a loving aunt and family.

The SS *Atlantis* was leaving very shortly for New Zealand, on 29 July 1949. I had been refused a place on it and was feeling very upset. I wrote to them, saying that they had led me to believe I would be accepted, and asking them to return my £10 and I would find my own way of getting there. The ship was sailing the next day and I hadn't heard anything, and while I was waiting anxiously, my manager, Mr Allen, said that no news could be good news. Later on that day they rang to say that they had reviewed my case, and as I had just met the criteria of 20 years of age, they would accept me. Joy of joys! I was to leave the next day from Tilbury Docks. There wasn't time to get a passport but they issued me with a Document of Identity.

I packed up my belongings, including my bicycle, and my aunt came to see me off at the London railway station from which I was to travel to Tilbury Docks. She ran after the train with tears running down her face – tears were running down mine, too. In the carriage was a group of young people, and the young man sitting opposite had a twinkle in his eye and seemed to be quite amused at my distress.

My cousins Marie and Danny were at the Docks to see me off but were behind a

Eleanor and the five women she shared a cabin with.

barrier as I had already been through customs. However, they passed me a farewell gift. A policeman who was on duty intercepted them, but luckily he let us off, as it was a genuine gift of a writing case.

The long and arduous voyage then began. It took nearly seven weeks to arrive in New Zealand as the SS *Atlantis* was an old Canadian hospital ship, sailing most of the way minus one of the four engines which broke down on the way. We sailed across the Australian Bight in mountainous seas.

There were 1000 single people on board, 600 young men and 400 women and, as you can imagine, we women were well sought after at dances so a lot of fun was had. (On the previous voyage the Captain had performed several marriages and he let it be known that this would not happen this time!) The conditions were not good on board, though: six bunks to each tiny cabin, and the food was terrible. I was already quite slim, yet I lost weight, so you can imagine how some of the young men fared. The only bread roll we had each day was at breakfast, and we pocketed that because they didn't give us anything for supper. There were no cordial type drinks through the tropics so water had to suffice. Tapioca puddings and the like were often served for pudding in the heat of the tropics, and only one piece of fruit was given on a Sunday for the whole week.

On the way we stopped for one day at each of Aden, Colombo and Fremantle, Perth. It was interesting to visit the various ports and passengers made sure that there were three people in the group with one male at least. At Perth they welcomed us with pipers leading us down the main street. They also gave us a ball.

The voyage was a very different experience from living in England (with very happy memories of childhood but a horrendous time in the war), and I was not often bored as there was always company. Nevertheless, the voyage was long and arduous, and I was very happy to reach our destination.

I arrived on 12 September 1949 and my mother and father were at the Wellington docks to meet me. We joined the Newman's bus which took us to Napier, stopping when it was getting dark at Woodville for dinner of "pea, pie and 'pud" [spud]. It was quite late by the time we arrived in Napier. I was very impressed with the palm trees that lined Kennedy Road because we didn't have palms in England and they looked so foreign and exciting. We were dropped off at George's Drive at my cousin Joan's house. She had a beautiful leg of pork ready for us. I couldn't believe my eyes when I saw the size of it, as when I left England food rationing was still in place.

After a week's recuperation from my travels I met Mr Dolbell, the Immigration Officer, who took me around to apply for a job. After deciding against Blyth's Fashion Store, he took me to Lawry Dowling and Wacher Solicitors. At that time Mr Dowling, who was also the local Mayor, already had someone, so I finished up working at the State Hydro Electric Co in the office of the storeroom employing all men. Funnily enough, a year later I had a phone call from Mr Dowling asking me to become personal secretary to Mr Weston Wacher. I really enjoyed working for Mr Weston Wacher.

Bill and Eleanor Patterson and family. 2002.

Music was my interest and I joined the Strollers musical club playing piano in a band. I also enjoyed ballroom dancing, cycling with my friends and swimming in the sea. New Zealand seemed to have a lot of clubs and activities. I found some of the expressions funny, for example, "doing his bun", "taking a plate" and a "cake of chocolate". I did miss Regent Street and Piccadilly in London, and the beauty of England.

A year or so later I met my future husband, Bill Patterson, married and lived in a complete change of lifestyle on a farm in Argyll, Waipawa.

Eleanor and Bill had five children and 14 grandchildren. During their married life they made two trips to England, both trips for holidays. When asked in 2008 if she had any regrets about coming to New Zealand, Eleanor stated categorically: "None whatsoever."

Illustrations acknowledgement

All photographs and other original material were supplied by Eleanor Patterson (nee Devine) and her daughter, Elysia Gumbley.

CHAPTER 3

John Parsons

Name	John Parsons
Ship	TSS *Captain Cook*
Departure date	19 August 1952
Arrival date	25 September 1952 (disembarked 26 September 1952)
Destination	North Island
Marital status	Single
Profession	Librarian
Intention	To return to England

John Parsons had already published his diary extracts in 2009 in a volume entitled *Gone to New Zealand*. He has kindly allowed me to reproduce material from his book.

On a June day in 1952 John received a bulky letter from New Zealand house in London at his home in Orpington. The letter contained sailing instructions for New Zealand.

Two things drove John to leave England. One was what he called his "itchy feet". The army had sent him first to Northern Ireland and then to India; and the thought of the chance to travel to New Zealand was not to be missed, especially as the contract with the New Zealand government promised free passage to New Zealand and demanded only a minimum two years in the job which had already been found for him. But the major reason was the death of his love, Elizabeth Stephenson, in 1950 – Orpington and Chislehurst carried too many painful memories of their time together there.

His diary account of the voyage was begun as a letter to Elizabeth, even though she had been dead for two years. He wanted to share with her the exciting kaleidoscopic nature of life aboard the TSS *Captain Cook* taking a thousand British and Irish immigrants of all ages to a new life in New Zealand.

John has since said, "The voyage helped ward off the pain. Also right from the beginning, starting at Euston Railway Station in London, on the boat train to Glasgow, it introduced me happily to Margaret Jones. We have been together ever since."

[21 June 1952]

A big, bulky, white letter came in the post from the Migration Offices. I picked it up and knew I was holding the future of at least the next two years. This was the confirmation of my baptismal visit to that little foyer in Pall Mall. I slit all the envelopes that had come and began to eat breakfast. Then with my mouth comfortably full, I took out the papers from the envelopes.

A warrant to Exeter, with compelling instructions, had come from the Army. The fishing article had come back. And I was to sail from Glasgow with just over 1000 migrants on the TSS *Captain Cook* on 19 August.

[17 August 1952]

Tomorrow, five years to the day since I came back to England, I start out on a fresh journey. Five years. And I am 25. A fifth of my lifetime ago? Then in a few minutes I shall be dead! So little done, so little hearsay shattered by experience. Everything is silent but the clamour of passing time, repeated three times here in the bedroom.

Mr and Mrs Stephenson came to tea and brought Elizabeth's travelling clock for me. I think it accompanied her everywhere. It is ticking over there by the window, echoing the one Miss Howe bought me, here on the bedside table. The third reminder is my watch. I can hear it ticking only if I lean a little nearer to the bedside table.

[17 August to 26 September 1952]

There is a little brown knee raised above the side of the pram just two yards away. The sun gleams on it. It belongs to a sun-browned baby with blonde hair who is sleeping soundly; sleeping through the chatter of people, the music that tumbles from the loudspeaker and the shrill shouts of little boys who tear along the narrow alleys left between the deck chairs.

SS *Captain Cook* says the blue label on the pram. There is another label, a round red one, with a K in the middle (K for Kuhlicke) that says "The New Zealand Shipping Company Limited". There is a third label, a striped blue and white one. The baby's mother, in a flowered cotton frock sits at one end of the pram knitting a pink woolly – but shouldn't it be blue? Mr Kuhlicke reads at the other end. Two men sit behind him on a piece of canvas-covered machinery playing Ludo. More men and girls sit around reading or sunbathing or strengthening three days' acquaintance.

There are 200 single women aboard. The dress varies from slacks and sweaters to cotton frocks. Some of the girls are glamorous and know it, and enhance their glamour with bright yellow or plum slacks and clinging black sweaters, a rag of magenta or jade scarf round their necks

The men are more conservative. At the moment they have got as far as open-necked shirts, slacks and sandals. Some have graduated to shorts, however, and some already have their shirts off and are browning under the hot and beneficial son. Beneficial because, especially to the English, constant sun is at once evocative of happiness and gaiety. The older men stick to blue and brown suits.

Everyone is emigrating to New Zealand. It seems that everyone is set on making a go of it. No one entertains the thought of judging the new country and the new people by an acquaintance of six months.

They are almost scornful of those who have gone before and who have scuttled back again to England after a few weeks, loud with grievances.

Taffy in our cabin is determined to stay. He says simply, in spite of our cautions, that he is not coming back. He will like it and that's all there is to say. He is going dairy farming. Another Welshman – a sheep farmer this time – is going back after the two years (of migrants' contracts), not to quit but to take back his girlfriend. He came up with me from London. His parting with the fair girl at Euston was tender yet passionate. The girl seemed anything but distraught. She was stealing glances at me out of beautiful eyes, whether from shyness or interest I could not quite determine.

The platform was crowded seven deep. Round red labels and blue and white labels, on the scores of cases that were carried along, proclaimed their destination. There were seats for all and there was space for even all the luggage that poured unceasingly onto the platform and into the carriages. Friends and relatives who had come to say goodbye knew that the parting was likely to be a long one, at least for two years, and yet only laughter and chatter filled the warm, dusky, grimy platform. Even at the end, at seventeen minutes past nine, when the train's departure irrevocably divided the people, there were few tears. For us who smiled comfortingly and then waved and waved, the parting was a release. We had been dreading these last few minutes. It was different for us, buoyed by excitement and an expectation of adventure that had built up slowly with the slowly moving machinery of emigration. Saying goodbye was perhaps even insignificant in that machinery, something that was to be escaped from if possible. But of course it was not possible.

Those who were left, waving, had only lived alongside the excitement. Theirs was a single emotion, empty of excitement, the emotion of truncated or suspended love or friendship.

The Welshman and I talked fishing. How close, and how soon, does fishing draw strangers together! There was a silence for some time in the carriage, however, following our departure. Now that we were actually embarked on the adventure, the business of leave-taking took on a deeper significance. In one corner was a dark-blue-eyed Irish girl. Opposite my corner was a brown-haired girl in glasses. She was not unattractive though her nose was a trifle sharp. She was assured and she turned out to be Welsh, not very noticeably. I panicked mildly later when she revealed that she too had come back to England five years ago to the day on the *Empire Trooper*. Even now, a week later, I can't tell whether she remembers me for what I was on that ship; an abnormally self-conscious (abnormal to neurosis) army officer wanting to do nothing but act and behave normally and failing miserably, as I had failed miserably since the enormous pressure of work two months before had overwhelmed me.

If she remembers – and she has made no sign – then she is determined to forget. I shall ask her. I thought everyone must have known. But perhaps that was only a part of my trouble.

In the train I thought she was a Margaret and she was. The oldest of the five of us, a thin haggard woman, sat between the Irish girl and Margaret. She was about 35. She looked like a Hilda (but turned out to be a Nora – not far out!) A little while after the train had started, another girl came in. She had a tiny case with a parcel tied to it and we soon found room for that between the others. She wore powerful glasses and from the first she was unmistakably Irish. Her nose was small and her nostrils were high.

We have learned a lot about her since that train journey. She is terrified of crowds because she is too self-conscious. With friends she feels less embarrassed. Alone with friends she is happiest. And yet she isn't shy. She has a grin that compels smiles. She speaks softly and she tells little stories against herself that make me shout with laughter. She is a little mad, charmingly so, and naive. The combination leads her into remarks that match her frown for seriousness, but that tickle us immensely. When we cannot conceal our amusement her grin suddenly appears from the frown and the I-hope-I'm-not-making-a-fool-of-myself expression. I could find no name for her and the other Irish girl but Mary, but she is Teresa (Terry for short), and the other is Josephine (Johanna actually, which became Josie).

Josie is quiet and given to daydreaming. From the first, in the train, even during the first few minutes when we thought quietly of the faces and the meaning of those going slowly now from Euston to the comfort of the pubs, there was something about Josie and that was not eloquent of chatter. The not-noticeably-Welsh girl Margaret broke the silence, saying something with a smile to the woman beside her. Then we were all talking and discovering what we were going out as, and exchanging our hopes and fears for the future. Josie's blue eyes reflected our laughter and anxieties. Later she talked too, but hesitantly. It was surprising how widely our reading of the official instructions differed. It was chiefly a matter of misinterpretation.

We slept in uncomfortable jerks; the boat-train had no sleeping cars. There was no restaurant car either. When we reached Carlisle however, about three in the morning, there was a restaurant open on the platform. Soon there was a long queue of tired, stiff and cold people eager for the warming paper cups of tea.

We were an hour late at Glasgow, arriving about 7.30am. After loading our luggage onto waiting lorries we were escorted to local restaurants by the WVS. [Women's Voluntary Service]. There were some complaints at the charge of 4/-, but on the whole, people took it calmly enough. Our meal was more than adequate.

The baby in the pram is awake. I thought it was a boy but it is a girl, so pink was the right colour. The sun is a little too strong for her I think. Her face is flushed and sleepy, and her father rocks the pram comfortingly.

In the lounges and smoking rooms there is a huge amount of gambling already. Pontoon is the favourite. Taffy won 35/- the first two days. How they can stay inside I can't understand, when outside a brilliant sun is shining, the sea rising and falling blue and white alongside and beyond, and a fresh, healthy breeze blowing. The bar opens at 11 and everyone wanting a drink then grabs a chair, for no one can go out and order but must be served by a steward. Standing people cannot order. This cuts out queuing and for that reason is a good system. Queues stretch for anything up to 40 yards for the canteen in the morning and afternoon.

I was sick immediately I awoke on the Wednesday morning – hardly out of the Clyde – and I was sick twice during the morning. I suppose sickness attacks even the most hardened sailors. I can hardly consider myself hardened, but an untroubled apprenticeship of two trips across the Bay of Biscay and four between Scotland and Ireland, I should have thought, would render me immune.

An entertainment committee was formed on Friday and that same evening there was Tombola in A Deck lounge. Half the prize for the first House was £2.12s. The lounge was packed into wicker chairs, and of course, there was queuing for the 'cards' (of paper, coloured blue or red or yellow, in books of counterfoils, three 'cards' to a page). There is queuing for everything, so ingrained into Britishers is the habit.

The canteen is open at 10am and again at 4pm. Cigarettes are 5s a 100, chocolate 6d an ounce. They sell all toilet articles, from toothbrushes to eau-de-cologne, films (2s3d), boiled sweets in cellophane packets, ink, writing paper, matches, Qwells [seasickness tablets], boot brushes, polish, etc.

We have to be out of our cabins by 9.30am so that the stewards can clear up for the daily inspection. Ours is a four-berth cabin, smallish, but containing two tiers of bunks, a wash basin, a cupboard, two chairs with upholstered seats and a chest of drawers (one drawer each). Two forced-draft vents solve the two problems of ventilation (there is no porthole; we are on C Deck), and drying out of 'smalls'. The vents are movable so that one can direct the draft where one likes. They are like balls (the size of bowling woods), with holes in the side: turned upwards they are closed. You are not supposed to dry out washing in front of them really (at least, it should not be on view for the morning inspection). B Deck is reserved for drying washing and when on B Deck aft, every day is Monday. Parallel strings have been tied up there and washing flaps all day long, washing that rarely drips because it dries out too quickly. Day by day it dries faster.

It is Sunday and church services have been held for Catholics and Protestants. It is no different from other days except that the canteen is closed. There was no traditional Sunday dinner. I had soup, York ham and salad, cheese and rolls, and coffee. I always have salad at lunch and nearly always at dinner, as light meals with raw vegetables are more suited to this weather than heavy meal courses.

The five of us (excluding Brian, who is probably gambling somewhere) have been sunbathing on the boat-deck most of the day. The sun has been potent. White caps with long peaks are popular. There is a Scotsman, one of 400 on board (who seems to be accompanying four women), who wears his light clothing amusingly. He has a yellow nylon shirt with a short zipper up the front, white, thick navy-blue shorts that come down to well below his knees, blue canvas sandals, and short white socks pulled up their full length. One morning he was sitting on deck with a woman's silk scarf tied fisher-girl style round his balding head, engrossed in some embroidery.

We have steamed 368 miles since noon yesterday and are now well past the Azores. The sea is calm, streaked with the smooth currents that bring up the round seaweed growths that surprised us at first so far out. In spite of the smooth sea a considerable swell rocks us. A school of porpoises undulates along the surface far out. It is 5.30pm and Brian has gone for two glasses of beer. He may not be successful: one must find a seat first. We must be at dinner at 6pm. There is trouble if you are late for meals. Not real trouble; but some of the stewards do not mind what they say to you; after all, aren't we just immigrants? Most of us think of them as stewards serving passengers on board ship. We are annoyed when they forget that they are in fact servants. They are drawing pay only for serving; good manners are not part of their work.

Sunset at sea can be glorious. Last night's showed us beauty of colour and cloud formation that the people lining the starboard rails had rarely seen before. There was a thin crescent of moon high up to the left. A long straightening procession of angry grey black clouds with tattered tops and a common base lay right across the western horizon. Above, yellowish orange diaphanous scarves and wisps and streaks of cloud hung across a deepening blue sky that turned almost cobalt above the just-invisible sun itself. An angry crimson tracing of cloud lingered like a frozen tongue of flame to mark the ending of the sun, a last defiant challenge to the moon.

The sun is blazing down today. It is brilliant and potent. Half an hour in it makes me feel a little ill: an hour might well make me sick. And yet the people crowding the decks in shorts and sun-tops embrace it hour after hour. It has ceased to be a beneficial sun. It's merciless. The crew, from today, must wear tropical kit – white shirts and shorts (or slacks), white socks and shoes, navy-blue epaulettes for the officers.

For several days now we have had flying fish periodically breaking the surface a few yards from the bows and flying out at right angles to the ship. They just skim the surface. I have not seen one longer than ten inches. The ones at that size, or nearest, travel quite quickly. We watched one, on the wrong tack altogether, escape from the ship by flying round the bows. We must have been doing fifteen knots ourselves. They are seen to their best effect in the lower rays of the morning sun. The light shines on their white under parts, and their vibrating fins look like dragonflies wings. Sometimes they skim the surface in their flight like swallows sipping nectar.

There have been occasional schools of porpoises, and a few whales spouting. Up to about Sunday there were sometimes long-winged seabirds flying just above the waves, similar to those that I remember seeing, I believe, in the Mediterranean. Are they skuas?

We miss natural colour. Days of ultramarine induce a longing for green grass and trees. The colours of tomatoes and lettuce, and the occasional apple and orange, are very restful. There is a remarkable variety in the colours of the clothes of course, but it's not the same as natural colour.

In the beginning, a week ago, we had the feelings and behaviour of a crowd embarked on a common adventure. That attitude is changing as friendships and cliques form. The smiles to others outside a particular circle are not so ready. Fours and fives of young men of the labouring type are less sympathetic, less careful of their behaviour and remarks than they were as strangers to one another a week ago. There is a faint antagonism towards other men who interest themselves in girls whom certain fellows have attracted. There is less tolerance of nuisances. We are reverting to type.

Three seagulls appeared just after midday, and now we are waiting for a sight of land – the island called Sombrero in the Antilles or Caribbean Isles. Last night was very humid, and today it is the same. I am wearing Indian sandals, brief swimming shorts, and Aertex shirt with short sleeves, and yet my whole body is uncomfortably sticky. But an hour sitting in the shade for'ard on the port side, where the breeze is to be felt the best, cooled me down to the point of discomfort, and I had to warm up again elsewhere.

Photo courtesy of Rosemary Burton

Curacao from the distance with many fuel storage tanks visible.

The children are given an hour's education each day. At 6am there is PT for men, followed by PT for women. Many exercise before breakfast on the boat deck, running round and round. Some rely on walking. I do myself. Before breakfast I walk a dozen times round the Promenade Deck, and again after dinner. I'm on their first sitting for meals – 7.45am breakfast, 12 noon lunch, 6pm dinner. Tea is served at 3 in the afternoon, but just a cup of tea and a single fairy-cake makes it hardly worth going down for. I'm glad I'm on the first sitting. Those on the second sitting who come on deck afterwards for deck chairs or folding 'arm-chairs' or folding stools are often disappointed – the later arrivals invariably.

The dock water of Willemstad looks like thin pea soup at 4.30 in the morning. We begin to refuel with heavy oil alongside the quay at 5 o'clock in the glare of orange fluorescent lights on the roofs of the trim white buildings a few yards away. The four dockies – or pump-men – were Jamaicans, in tattered clothes and old hats. What surprised me most were the ten dogs on the quay like degenerate foxhounds, neither scratching nor howling nor fighting. A dark patch of waste oil began to spread out on the pea-soup on the port side.

It got light quickly. Beyond the round silver Shell storage tanks perched on the high ridge – hardly a cliff – opposite, light swelled into the sky.

First a whisper of cloud turned pink, then the sky went pale blue. A bird, roosting in the low flat-topped trees clothing the steep side of the ridge, called clearly. It was rather like a thrush. The brown road at the base of the ridge is about 200 yards away across the pea soup. One or two odd concrete structures stand there, and one or two derelict-looking barges lie in the water. Further along to the right is the first quay, where a small tanker lies. Above it a long brown warehouse huddled against the ridge, with the words "Curacao Trading Company, S.A." on it in large white letters. Five tankers went quietly past before I went down to the cabin for my cup of tea.

At the left-hand end of the quay road stood a group of single-storey yellow buildings with red roofs. All the while I was on deck they blazed with lights, and were loud with South American music. It was obviously an all-night party. Later a bevy of dusky girls in bright dresses left the buildings and strolled back along the road. The fuel-oil smell was sickening. There was no other air to be had, of course, and the forced-draft machinery was filling the cabins with it too.

There was an announcement after breakfast to the effect that all passengers could go ashore till 11pm. No spirituous liquors were to be brought on board. The Dutch and Jamaicans were friendly and generous people, and it was hoped that we should preserve our good name as passengers of the *Captain Cook* by not offending anybody. The sailor in the next cabin poked his head around the door.

"Going ashore, men? Don't forget, if you want any Duropacks or French letters I've got some next door. Right?"

"Yes," I grinned.

So that was wine and women brought into focus. Song came later, put into rhythmical focus by a little group of calypso players in a small bar. One guitarist looked South American and the other almost a Negro. This man wore a brilliant multi-coloured shirt. Charlie, one of the passengers, a small Jewish-looking bald man with a face like a parrot when he sings, was contributing to the entertainment. According to his card, his name in the world of London party and wedding entertainment is Buddy Bing Rogers.

Maduro's wharf, Curacao.

Photo courtesy of Phyllis Young

There was just half an hour to go before we had to be back at the ship, and several passengers had stopped on the way back to listen. Margaret, who does not disguise a rather critical and intolerant outlook, particularly on occasions when entertainment is understood to be amateur, groaned and rolled her eyes when Charlie sang. She wanted to hear some calypso.

A tall black Jamaican with a brown Homburg came in. The barman found a ukulele for him, and with an occasional quick grin that showed his awareness of us, he began to tune up.

The harmony of the day, metaphorically now, was almost as complete as that between Charlie the Englishman's singing and that Calypso group. I suppose most of the 1000- odd passengers went ashore at some time. A few returned merry, but not as drunk as some of the crew, who caused hard things to be said of them I've no doubt by the natives, who preserved invariably expressionless faces at the instant of a brawl or insult.

Shops opened for us (it was a Sunday) and remained open in some cases until well after half past nine.

Willemstad's prosperity comes from oil. What immediately strikes you on a walk through the town is the incredible number of luxurious American cars. The shiny bodywork on a stationary car gets so hot you could fry an egg on it. One car I saw had a fan alongside the steering wheel. Curacaon traffic uses the right-hand side, so we had to be careful, particularly as fast driving is a characteristic of the people. Fast turning at corners gave rise to a squeal of tyres that was continuous – and frightening for us. Horns were continuous too.

It was an immaculate town – immaculate in dress and food hygiene. The streets were almost immaculate too. Obviously the Dutch had introduced their code of cleanliness to the town, a code that made an instant appeal to me. Whether the fact of its being a Sunday affected the nature of the natives' dress I do not know, but it was undeniable that every Jamaican wore clean clothes. The bias towards American styles is important only because it rights a misconception: Jamaicans in Soho are not overdressed, according to their standards. Neatly creased gaberdine trousers and multicoloured bowties were especially popular.

There was nothing blowsy or untidy about the girls who lingered, unsmiling, at the corners towards evening and afterwards. A pair of American spectacles seemed to be an essential part of their dress – but they weren't advertising optical equipment. I thought of the sailor who had come prepared.

Colour seemed in integral part of Willemstad. The houses, more noticeably in the residential area, were often a crude red-brown or green. Nora observed that there were no chimney pots. A Jamaican on a Charing Cross train would be aware of certain things about our living conditions – the crowdedness, the grime, the forest of chimney pots. While in Willemstad we were aware of cleanliness (relative squalor fringed the town of course), bright tiled roofs uninterrupted by chimney pots, designs in white on the coloured front of houses, archways, slim columns arising from verandahs, the rarity of glass windows but the prevalence of shuttered windows backed with fine gauze, palms and brilliantly flowered shrubs in the gardens. Clearly Willemstad was a hot place and continued hot throughout the year.

It was excessively hot at midday and during the afternoon. We chose this time to stroll. The girls suffered. The shopping centre is on one side of the waterway that leads to the docks, the show-front on the other. A swing-bridge joins the two. This is at least 200 yards long. It is pushed across by an engine presumably driving a screw, like a ship. A clock each end tells you when next the bridge will be available to travel across. Ships must invariably upset the timetable. We went across on the 12.05 trip.

Some of the shop windows in the main street were beautifully dressed. Artistically, they exceed the taste of those in Oxford Street. Bond Street would consider itself honoured if one or two of the jewellers' shops were put down in it.

The name 'Seamen's Home' belies the near-magnificence of the building near the waterfront. Nearly all the passengers – in fact, every one of them I should think – visited the place at some time during the day. The Salvation Army equivalent was considerably less attractive, though that was probably not the opinion of the children from the ship, who were vastly entertained by the monkey and his little kennel on top of a pole in the yard at the back.

We were impressed, being British, and a little proud, to find that so many people spoke English, and that signs on shops in other places were usually in English. The first of the five languages saying 'Seamen's Home' on the board outside the building was in English too.

There was a shop inside the place as well as two bars and a restaurant. Sleeping accommodation for sailors was presumably on the next and higher floors. We had been told that about the only place that would not overcharge us was the Seamen's Home. Most people went there for drinks and souvenirs. All drinks were bottled. Pepsi-Cola was very popular, at 15 cents a bottle. Lemonade and orangeade were 20 cents, rum 40 cents. It was cheaper to drink rum – a pale powerful rum (86% proof) than beer. Beer – Pilsener lager – was 70 cents a bottle. It could have been a very expensive day for us. Visitors from ships always suffer because the amount of money they have is based on costs and salaries at home. Cost in salaries in Willemstad were extremely high. Four guilders 20 cents to the pound sterling made beer at 70 cents four shillings a pint. Broken ice was a necessity in each drink. I could sing that song "Drinking Rum and Coca-Cola ..." with experience behind it now. I was determined not to leave without drinking at least one. Cheese or meat sandwiches were 30 cents. The barmen were English-speaking Dutchmen, other servants Jamaican. Postcards at 10 cents each seemed exorbitantly expensive, particularly – illogically – those printed in Great Britain. Airmail postage for them amounted to 25 cents each – plus 15 cents for the Seamen's Home if you bought the stamps there.

Photo courtesy of Rosemary Burton

Curacao town as seen from the TSS *Captain Cook*.

Houses and shops on both sides of the waterway made a really colourful show. Dutch flags fluttering along the bridge added more colour.

We left Willemstad on Monday evening at 6.30. Gradually the geography of the town was made ridiculously clear. As we had wandered in the afternoon, virtually lost, our ship had seemed miles off. We could have seen it from the other side of the swing-bridge – just poked away round the corner.

It may have been the unaccustomed exercise of the previous day or the accumulated exhaustion of days of humid heat, that made me feel suddenly depressed. Life seemed flowing by as fast and heedlessly as the blue and white sea. But I knew beyond question that what I was doing was right for me.

Now that we had left the pea-soup of Willemstad and were out on the uncontaminated sea again, we could have our showers again. Someone thoughtfully left them full on for a time to wash the pipes clean of the oil and pea-soup, but the strong garlic smell lingered for hours.

Later on Monday night an isolated terrace of lights made its appearance to starboard. We passed it slowly and wrinkled our noses in disgust at the putrid breeze that came from it.

At 3 o'clock on Wednesday afternoon a faint grey silhouette, hardly distinguishable from the clouds, appeared to the south. Slowly it took on substance, developing into a distinct land high with hills. By 5 o'clock it was sufficiently near for us to be able to distinguish depth – to see different ranges of ridges and mountains. For a long time the eastern extremity towards which we were headed was shrouded with cloud.

When the sun appeared we were passing a rugged peninsula and a few small green islands rising abruptly from the sea. The faraway hills in the sunlight seemed covered in green candlewick material. Then it was time to change for dinner. We passed the flashing light on the seaward end of the long mole that reaches out from Cristobal and took a pilot and other officials aboard. Then began a long wait while, with engines reversed, we backed slowly towards the distant lights of another town across the water from Cristobal.

"We shall never get ashore at 9 at this rate," observed someone.

"Perhaps we're going to anchor out here all night," gloomily answered someone else.

People were filling the decks, having changed into collars and ties – even suits – and dresses more appropriate to the occasion than to the usually warm evening aboard. We had been warned that Cristobal was a tough city, that it was prudent to go about in groups, and that it was unwise to wander off the main streets. Women were strongly advised not to carry bags with shoulder straps; a man with a razor could slash the straps in a moment and be lost in the crowd. Excited chatter and laughter sounded everywhere to hide the flicker of apprehension that the announcement caused. People quickly made up small parties. I didn't want to risk being the only male (a slight one at that!) in a party of six, so I contacted a gang of five chaps (two of whom came from Ashford incidentally), and arranged for our party to accompany them.

At last the cause of our withdrawal was apparent; another ship crossed our bows and slipped quietly away into the night.

We berthed about half-past eight at Pier G, alongside a huge white building like a warehouse. People begin to queue to go ashore, as we were to be back on board by midnight.

Although it was dark, the dock-lights at once made us aware of the incredibly smooth trunks and feather-duster tops of a line of palms edging the road peak.

Before we had walked as far as the harbour-police post (where American police cursorily examined our International Certificates of Vaccination), tall white buildings on the right-hand side of the road drew remarks appreciative of their cool looks and their balconies set with ornamental palms.

The throb of music accompanied our wandering. Most insistent was the boom of double basses. A large illuminated vertical sign advertised the Copocabana Club, and smaller signs other clubs or saloons less pretentious. What streets we saw were very much alive. Not only were all the bars open, but most of the shops as well – especially the kind that sold curios and souvenirs. The bars were reminiscent of those in Western films – particularly the several entrances each with a swing door. They were roomy and rather dimly-lit.

The rate of exchange varied among the shops. At one we were quoted $2.50, and at another $2.20. The average was $2.40. We were careful to ascertain that we were getting an exchange of at least $2.40 before we bought anything. In most of the souvenir shops alligator (or crocodile) leather-ware was conspicuous and

Photo courtesy of Phyllis Young

Pilot coming aboard the TSS *Captain Cook* at Cristobal.

cheap. A small lady's bag-cum-wallet was only $2.00. Leather belts – some of them beautifully made – varied from $1.00 to $3.00. I bought myself one costing $1.50. Postcards were 10 cents each but I got a packet of 24 for half a dollar. These souvenir shops were open air; that is, their counters often opened straight onto the street. Several entrances gave the impression that you were walking round two or three shops at once.

The atmosphere of the town was less pleasant than that of Willemstad. One could indeed imagine bag-snatching as attaining the proportions of a profitable industry for some of the men walking about. There were no dogs to be seen, and that was puzzling. Hardly any of the locals were smoking. Those who were chewed cigars. One passenger scoured the town for a tobacco-pouch, without success.

Bananas came aboard in dozens. One bunch had to be carried by two men, and at a distance they looked to be carrying a drunk. A rumour circulated about the bananas: they were full of red ants. Denis, one of our cabin-mates, heard about this quite early. Seeing Bob with a large bunch he told him that he wasn't to bring any bananas into his cabin. Bob is Irish, with a head like an egg and a wide toothy grin. He had been sampling the liqueur of Christabal. Moreover, his conversation with friends had been rudely interrupted. Furthermore, Bob is self-righteous, and he was also getting well into a bout of vaccine-fever. The scene in the cabin afterwards was without blood, but only just without. They would feel different in the morning, despite promises to throw each other overboard.

On September 4 we were still berthed at Colon. Apparently ships do not travel through the Panama Canal by night. It was raining heavily. At 11am we reversed from the pier, then went forward, turning to starboard.

The first part of the journey until 12.30pm lay through a wonderland of lakes and heavily-foliaged islands. Then Gatun Lock; long low cable cars – dark grey picked out with yellow – running on central ratchet rails, waiting to control our run into the loch, four on each side. Hawsers came aboard, and then began the delicate work of squeezing us, unscratched, into the narrow channel, edging us foot by foot towards the gates. Americans in long-peaked caps controlled the cars, one in each cab.

Above us four ships were queuing to go back the other way, and we seemed to rise about thirty feet to get on their level.

We got to the next lock, the Pedro Miguel, about 4.30pm. Between these two the canal is a canal now – a narrow channel of water sometimes only three widths of the ship wide. The banks were high. Dumpy hills rose behind them, obscured at times by dragging watery clouds. It stopped raining close on 3 o'clock and the sun made the hills and the jungle-lined waterway beautiful. Some trees were tall, with gracefully-drooping branches, some ugly with stumpy branches. There were feathery palms. There were patches of plants with long wide leaves and spikes of bright orange flowers. There were tall trees whose thin trunks seemed to have been partially whitewashed.

A line of palms edging the road near the docks at Cristobal.

Photo courtesy of Phyllis Young

If they were not swallows that went to and fro alongside, then they were very like them. Tern-like birds passed too. The feeling of being on a moving platform miraculously cleaving the jungle was enhanced by the insects that flew across. Occasionally a waterfall broke the greenery, very often white and black-striped squares of wood; rarely a wooden hut.

While at dinner we passed through another lock. I looked up to see a face framed in the porthole. One of the cable-car drivers was looking in at us from his cab. It was dark then, and at Balboa really dark except for the lights.

The Atlantic had adopted the character of the Pacific, and the Pacific is behaving as though it is the Atlantic. Since yesterday morning, when we drew away from the ghostly grey coast of Panama, the sea has been, to us, heavy. The ship has never rolled like this before. A forceful wind drives up occasional showers of spray on the Promenade Deck for'ard. Grey skies brightened sometimes by sunshine prevail. The Atlantic crossing was serene.

Eleven days from Wellington the ship was stark black and stark white under a tropical sun. The gleaming black bows cleft the waves hungrily and the sun struck the baffled impotence of the water a blinding white. Flicking from the waves went the flying fish, terrified of the monstrous creature descending on them. In the air they caught fire from the sun. They glittered like silver sparks until the sea received them again, quenching them.

Up on a white lifeboat two old men in blue jerseys screwed up their faces at the glare from the sea and the sky. They are refurbishing aluminium-coloured blocks with yellow ropes, harsh and creaking with newness. Shrill happiness arose from

Pedro Miguel Locks, Panama.

Photo courtesy of Phyllis Young

Photo courtesy of Phyllis Young

Mules at the Pedro Miguel Locks.

the children's canvas paddling pool below them, but they did not look down. As the ship rolled, waves accelerated by the shrieking children slopped over the sides of the pool, provoking mock horror or pleasant benevolence in the older people, who pushed the gaily-coloured canvas chairs further back into the crowd.

The younger men and girls lay back, languid and brown, intent only on devouring more and more sun. They had begun to devour it two days out from Glasgow. Now, three weeks of strangely uncharacteristically hot and serene Atlantic and strangely cool and rolling Pacific later, they were as brown as the deck itself.

Young and old on board had a brownness in common, a new life ahead in New Zealand in common, and the look of being British in common … a thousand of them, strong, healthy, sweating; married and unmarried; herd-testers and typists, sheep-shearers and clerks, printers, nurses and servicemen, and seventy other kinds of worker besides. The single men outnumbered the single women by more than two to one, and yet restraint and understanding rarely collapsed. When it did, because of too much beer, or too much heat, or maladjusted leisure, the unpleasantness was brief.

Elizabeth would have loved all of it. She would have loved the thousand of us, from Mary the little Scots girl who paraded up and down crying out in a beautiful voice "Deck chairs needed!" to Charlie, the stooping, Jewish-looking (and depraved-looking) self-appointed entertainer to us all, who looked like a bald-headed parrot when he sang. She would have discovered even Charlie's better nature, and shown us all. I wouldn't have envied her the limelight that must have bathed her before

35

long. It would have been more than enough just to have had her there. She was, incomprehensibly to me, both pleased and unaffected by popularity. I would have begrudged her nothing, well aware that what popularity I might have enjoyed myself would have been simply a reflection of hers, as Elizabeth's friend. Friend? But I could not think of myself as her lover. I had loved her, but that love had never had physical confirmation. Flying fish leapt from the blue, but I saw only the blue of the bluebell park shadowed by the sturdy tree with the plaque on it in the crematorium.

At last, a thousand miles from Wellington, the rough seas came. The ship see-sawed and rolled through a long irregular swell dancing with foaming wave-crests. A tearing wind hurled delicate bellows of lace from the crests. The taut wires soaring skywards about the masts sang a booming song, and over all the wild agitation of sea and ship a brilliant sun shone. The card-players and the drinkers stuck stubbornly to the windless smoky lounges. Some were sick below. Some, in thicker clothes, sat about in sheltered corners on the decks. Some, in raincoats, went for'ard, exulting in the clamour and plunge of steel and sea.

The leaping, shaking decks lent force to an air of excitement enclosing the ship that particular afternoon. Ingenuity of mind and fingers were engaged in the test of devising costumes out of practically nothing for the carnival dance that night. An astonishing number of people were concerned in the making and lending of clothes and dresses. I lent a tie and a shirt and a pair of socks to Nora, who had borrowed a suit, hat, and briefcase to go as a business man. Josie gave me dark face-powder for my role as Indian-cum-sheik. One couple and three friends spent the entire morning cutting out cardboard discs from old menus and covering them with a silver paper salvaged from cigarette tins. They went as the Pearly King and Queen. Pirates were popular, but there was only one nun. Disguised simply and effectively in a sheet, sandals, and turban, iodine over my face and burnt cork moustache and eyebrows, I felt quite staid against the dozens of incredibly original costumes parading along the decks before going below to the judges.

The succession of 'last dances' had just ended when the Liaison Officer dramatically announced that a faint beacon light off the starboard bow was to be seen – the ship's first visual contact with New Zealand. People at that moment had their hands linked for 'Auld Lang Syne': the next moment they rushed for the rails.

The next day, September 25, 1952, in a squally southerly, the *Captain Cook* dropped anchor in Wellington Harbour, and a thousand new arrivals from the other end of the world looked at the shore and the city rising from it, and the surrounding hills gay with little coloured roofs, and wondered what was in store for them.

Once interviews and other formalities were completed the following day, and the ship was finally berthed, we said goodbye to the *Captain Cook* and went ashore to begin new lives in New Zealand.

I would be 26 the next day.

Some two years after arriving in New Zealand, John married Margaret Jones, the Welsh woman he met on the London to Glasgow train. John and Margaret remained in New Zealand where they raised three children who, in their turn, gave John and Margaret eight grandchildren. John returned to England once, 46 years after arriving, to visit his daughter and her family.

John's recollections of what he knew about New Zealand before emigrating were of a land with an unspoilt environment; and trout fishing. Prior to leaving England he had already had some articles on fishing published in England. He lives at Taupo and continues to publish books on fishing in New Zealand.

Illustrations acknowledgement

Except where otherwise acknowledged, all photographs and other original material were supplied by John Parsons.

CHAPTER 4

Alma Evans

Name	Alma Evans
Ship	*Rangitoto*
Departure date	5 September 1952
Arrival date	6 October 1952
Destination	North Island
Marital status	Single
Profession	Cook

In September 1952 my parents and all but two of my family left Wales for New Zealand for a better lifestyle. My oldest brother had immigrated to New Zealand three years earlier and Gwyneth, the last of us seven children, immigrated three years later.

All I really knew about New Zealand before coming was that it had a small population and a better climate. We travelled from Wales to London and sailed from Tilbury Docks.

A stormy day on the voyage. Alma on board the *Rangitoto*.

Alma and Ted Lawrence on their wedding day.
11 July 1953.

Aside from leaving the boat for a few hours at each end of the Panama Canal we remained on board the whole trip. To keep us amused on board we had deck games, dances and concerts. Early in the morning we walked around the deck. My sister, three brothers and I formed close relationships with other young people but only stayed in touch for a few years after the trip. I did not get bored on the trip – I found it exciting. It was my first big adventure after a sheltered home life and the restrictions of the War.

I recall feeling both excitement and some trepidation as we got closer to New Zealand.

When we arrived we were met by my brother and two friends who drove us to our new home where there was a very warm welcome for us at the village hall.

I soon started my new job in Stratford, Taranaki, at a boarding school for girls. Quite different circumstances to what I was used to. I worked long hours, starting early to light the coal range and get the porridge going. A close watch was kept on any wastage in the kitchen. I was told once that the girls were wasting potatoes by peeling them too thickly. The housekeeper had very little knowledge of a balanced menu and I didn't like what I had to cook, being used to a higher standard of food for the pupils. The first batch of scones I baked at the school, I used half lard, half butter, and I was told off for using lard – I was so used to rations and only having two ounces of butter a week.

I slept in a small hut on the premises. One night I was scared stiff on finding a very large insect in my bed – it attached itself to my hair. I tried killing it with my shoe but its shell was too hard.

I enjoyed the social activity in New Zealand. My father was a very keen Presbyterian and forbade frivolous activities and events so I enjoyed the freedom in New Zealand. Coming from Wales, though, I did miss the singing. Leisure activities were mainly dancing or tramping. I particularly remember the dances where the men all stood around the door and the women were seated around the walls. Soon after arriving I met my husband in a dance at Stratford and we were married before I'd been here one year.

Alma and Ted went on to have four children and six grandchildren. Like many other women in rural areas, Alma joined her local branch of WDFF (Women's Division of Federated Farmers – now Rural Women New Zealand) in 1969, and is still a member 40 years later. Then, as now, RWNZ provided support and friendship for women who would otherwise have been very isolated. For some women, RWNZ also provided opportunities to take on leadership roles in the community and Alma was one of those. Toko Branch is part of Central Taranaki Provincial and Alma joined the Provincial in 1975 and in 1982 went on to lead the Provincial for four years as Provincial President. Her years of community service were recognised by the Provincial in 1988 when Alma was made a Member of Honour, and again in 1993 when she was made a Life Member.

© bedwar ban byd

The Evans family

Celebrating 50 years in New Zealand

October 1952 - October 2002

On September 5, 1952, the Evans Family - parents, Thomas and Lydia , Alma, Ieuan, Emrys, Iola and Dewi - sailed to their adopted country aboard the Rangitoto.

A large crowd of family and friends were at the Llandudno Junction Railway station to bid them farewell as they boarded the overnight train to London.

Tudor, the eldest, had emigrated to New Zealand three years earlier and Gwyneth came out three years later.

There were mixed feelings on leaving, but great excitement on boarding the ship for the four week voyage through the Panama Canal and arriving in New Zealand four weeks later on October 6.

Wellington harbour, on a clear bright morning was a wonderful sight as they sailed in.

Tudor and two friends, John Binne and Johnny Jones were there to meet the family and welcome them. After sorting out documents and luggage the family travelled in three cars to Huinga in Taranaki.

A welcome party was held in the Huinga Hall soon after they arrived and the family sang a few light songs together.

Members of the family went their separate ways - to jobs, and Dewi to school at Stratford.

They are all now married to New Zealanders and settled in different parts of the country, but whenever they get together, there is always singing.

The boys have sung together at functions, and Ieuan is in great demand as a soloist and sings in three different choirs.

A Welsh TV documentary was made about the family in 1994 presented by Dai Jones in the *Cefn Gwlad* series.

There are now 27 grandchildren and 42 great grandchildren. Thomas and Lydia, Tudor, Gwyneth, Emrys' wife Trish, and Alma's husband Ted have, however, all passed away, and are greatly missed.

This contribution was first published in *Yr Enfys, journal of Undeb Cymru a'r Byd* [The Journal of Wales International] in October 2002.

Illustrations acknowledgement

All photographs and other original material were supplied by Alma Lawrence (nee Evans).

CHAPTER 5

Carol Symington

Name	Carol Joy Symington
Ship	TSS *Captain Cook*
Departure date	10 December 1952
Arrival date	14 January 1953
Destination	South Island
Age	9

December 10, 1952, was my ninth birthday. Feeling seasick I stood on the deck of the *Captain Cook*, looking over the rail, as we sailed down the Irish Sea heading for New Zealand. It was very exciting. I knew that we were going a long way away, and most probably there were those among the passengers who were in tears as they waved good-bye to those on the wharf at Glasgow, but I don't remember them. I had total trust in my father, and I suppose I had caught his optimistic attitude to the voyage. In my mind we were setting out on a wonderful adventure. My father, Ralph, had been in the Royal Navy. He had always wanted to go to sea, but being the youngest in his family, had felt obligated to stay with his widowed mother. However, he enlisted in 1939, not long before the start of the war. He signed up for a 12 year term and so served in the navy throughout the war. During these dreadful years of war, my mother, Marion, never knew if she would see her husband again. My parents had met in Leicester, and married in 1940. During the course of the war they had two daughters, Shirley and me, Carol. When the war ended my father was stationed ashore in both Malta and Gibraltar. But he had become disenchanted with naval life. The death of his mother in 1946, and the birth of my brother Ralph in 1948, led to him to apply for compassionate leave and this was granted. He resumed life in Leicester, working in a hosiery factory, but had to remain ready for call-up until his 12 year term was up in 1951.

During his time in the navy Dad had developed a desire to leave England. I've always thought this was due mainly to an adventurous spirit and "itchy feet" from his time in the Navy. I believe he also had an aversion to the class system that he had experienced while in the Navy. (On his own merits he had risen to be Chief Petty Officer and he was proud of that achievement. But ships officers at that time were from the upper class and Dad's working class background meant that

Carol Symington on board the TSS *Captain Cook*.

he could never aspire to be an officer.) A few years ago my mother told me that the main reason we left was the common fear at the time that there could be nuclear war in Europe. And post-war Britain was not an appealing place. I remember my mother having a ration book. She used to trade her stocking coupons for sugar. My sister had asthma, and there were coupons for her orange juice which was dispensed at the hospital. I can remember the first time my father came home with a chocolate bar. It was a very rare treat, and the Mars Bar was cut into four pieces for us to share. So in many ways leaving for a new life in another country seemed desirable.

When I was about seven years old my father took a new job to the north in Middlesborough. Now our table was often covered with pamphlets about various Commonwealth countries. My Uncle who lived in South Africa would not sponsor us to join him – no place for children, he wrote. I can remember my Mum and Dad discussing Canada – too cold, they decided. For a while they were considering Queensland, until my mother found out about the snakes and spiders and crocodiles – I can remember her quite definitely declining to move there! Eventually, they chose New Zealand. By now it was 1952 and my father had been released from naval service. One day he came home and told us he had been interviewed by someone from New Zealand. The representative of the Mosgiel Woollen Mills was in England to recruit skilled workers for the factory. Dad was offered a job, signed up for two years, and was accepted as an immigrant. And so we became "£10 Poms".

A few possessions were packed into two or three suitcases. (There must have been a trunk as well which went into the hold of the ship.) Our furniture was sold,

Carol, Marion, Ralph Junior and Shirley Symington on the deck of the TSS *Captain Cook*.

and our remaining goods were spread out on the lounge floor for people to buy. My mother said one dealer got most and paid very little. This would have been furniture and other things that she had inherited from her parents. We got a train to Leicester to say good-bye to our relatives, and stayed with one of Dad's sisters and her family. We must have been there in November, since I remember seeing a bonfire in the street and fireworks, and we had sparklers to write our names with. There were many emotions in play that time – as a child I was aware of the stresses and especially of my mother's upsets. I can't remember us visiting her brothers and friends to say good-bye, but I do remember the farewell party that was held at my aunt and uncle's house. There were streamers and special food, but also many tears from my father's relatives. I remember his sister hugging Dad and crying and saying, "Ralph, we won't ever see you again." The next day we set out on the train for Glasgow. We were in a compartment and it must have been a night train and cold, since Mum tucked us up in blankets and we slept in our coats on the seats. I can't remember actually boarding the *Captain Cook*, but I can recall being on board among a lot of people. My father went off to register the family for meals, but he got in late and we got the second sitting. This meant by the time we got on deck after lunch it could be hard to find seating on the crowded decks.

My mother, sister and brother and I shared a four-berth cabin, while our father, I believe, was in some sort of dormitory with other men. In the Maritime Museum in Auckland there is a mock-up of a cabin of a 1950s immigrant ship. It is based on a Dutch ship, but is very similar to how I remember our cabin.

What did I do all day? My memory is hazy but certain incidents do stand out.

… Going ashore at Curacao. It was hot and there were lovely tropical flowers and dark people. We went to the swimming pool, which was the first time I had ever had such an enjoyable experience. I loved it. I have a photo which shows us wearing wooden life jackets. I wonder where we got swim suits?

I remember going through the Panama Canal and seeing islands covered with green jungle and bright birds. And going through the huge locks. At Panama City we went ashore at night. It was Christmas Eve and there were lots of "happy" people around, and the police had guns. In a shop window there was a translucent plastic half-leg lit up by a light inside on which was displayed the latest in seamed stockings. Very glamorous. My father and his friends got very drunk and came back late, and my mother was upset.

"Crossing the line" was on 27 December 1952. Water was splashed on us and I got a certificate from King Neptune.

One day the ship's siren was sounded and the ship went about. I stood at the rail and watched the half circle white wake as we turned around. A woman was in the sea and was recovered and taken aboard. There were rumours that she may have jumped overboard, or maybe she just fell in. Someone had thrown her a lifebuoy. In the Pacific I stood at the rail and watched flying fish, and lovely sunsets.

We saw some movies. I remember one about New Zealand where the scenes of Christchurch included shots of hundreds of cyclists and hardly any cars, and a newsreel which showed President Eisenhower giving a speech which I think must have been at his inauguration. My mother was very dismissive of his style, saying, "That's typical of Americans". I suppose we had picked up some newsreels and movies in Panama.

As it got hotter and hotter I developed hives (my reaction to heat throughout my early life), so my mother took me to the ship's doctor. He was a nasty man. He said to my mother, "You people must learn to keep your children clean." In those days you didn't talk back to doctors or question them, but I remember my mother being very quiet and stiff as we left. We were always well looked after; Mum made our dresses and constantly knitted cardigans and jerseys for us and brushed our hair every day and I knew this doctor was wrong to say what he did. What sort of doctor travelled on these ships?

There were some Greek immigrants on the ship. One of the women was very fond of my sister and me, and she used to help Mum plait our hair. I think this family settled in Wellington and ran milk bars.

After days and days of nothing but the sea we saw an island. It was Pitcairn Island. As we got closer we saw a boat being rowed towards us. Mother told me it was because the sea was too rough to go nearer, and the people were trying to reach us to sell us souvenirs. However, we sailed past.

At last in mid-January 1953 we arrived at Wellington. People gathered along the rails for their first view of this place. I was standing next to Mum and she was very quiet. In one of his plays Roger Hall has a great description of what they were seeing and how he felt. The small wooden houses perched on the hills looked

Carol's Crossing the Line
Certificate.

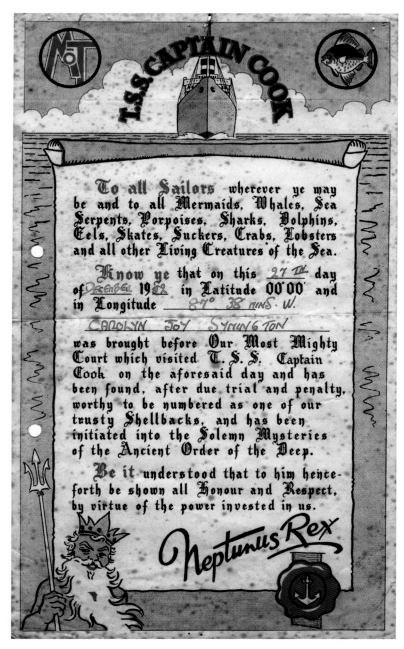

T.S.S. CAPTAIN COOK

To all Sailors wherever ye may be and to all Mermaids, Whales, Sea Serpents, Porpoises, Sharks, Dolphins, Eels, Skates, Suckers, Crabs, Lobsters and all other Living Creatures of the Sea.

Know ye that on this _27TH_ day of _December_ 19_52_ in Latitude 00°00' and in Longitude _87° 38 mins. W._

CAROLYN JOY SYMINGTON

was brought before Our Most Mighty Court which visited T. S. S. Captain Cook on the aforesaid day and has been found, after due trial and penalty, worthy to be numbered as one of our trusty Shellbacks, and has been initiated into the Solemn Mysteries of the Ancient Order of the Deep.

Be it understood that to him henceforth be shown all Honour and Respect, by virtue of the power invested in us.

Neptunus Rex

strange to me. It had been raining, and there were very few people around. Quite a shock for people who had come from the big industrial cities of England!

We went ashore, and had a ride on the cable car. Then we boarded the night ferry to Lyttelton. From Lyttelton we went by train to Dunedin. The whole train must have been full of immigrants, since we stopped for a sit-down lunch at (I think) Ashburton. The tables were covered with white tablecloths, and someone made a speech of welcome. From the Dunedin station we walked a short distance to the Early Settlers Hall where a nice woman welcomed us to New Zealand. I can't remember how we got to Mosgiel. There used to be a train, but we may have been taken there by car.

The Woollen Mills management was to provide a house, but renovations were not complete, so we went to live in a room at the Mill hostel. Dad bought furniture; rimu drawers and beds, which my parents used all their lives. We children had a great time while we lived there, since we used to get into the huge shed where the wool bales were kept and climb on them and use them as slides.

Eventually we moved into the small house and then started school. It was summer and the sky was blue and clear. I made friends with a group of girls as soon as I started school, even though at first they made fun of my accent. On the weekends we would head out into the countryside on our bikes. I thought it was great to be in New Zealand.

However, this new life was a terrible shock to my mother, and from the first days of our arrival she wanted to go back home. I remember during the first few days going with her to buy groceries, and at that time the shop had sacks of flour and blocks of butter which the shopkeeper cut up to order. She thought this was very primitive. The house that had been provided was a very basic small wooden place with a coal stove. Mosgiel was a small quiet place after the big cities she had left. She missed her family and friends and was very unhappy. My father had started work and began to make friends with other immigrants who also worked at the Mill. There were many Friday night parties, which my mother did not like. A couple they had met on the *Captain Cook* were living in Dunedin, and they remained friends and we used to visit them at the grocery shop they had bought, but Mum remained very unhappy and I remember her often being in tears. Then Dad would tell her that when he had served his two-year bond we would go back to England.

My sister Lesley was born in Mosgiel in 1957, and I would say this eventually helped my mother to settle. After Dad's two-year contract was served they did not return to England. I guess they did not have the money to go. Instead, in 1958, the family moved to Christchurch. My parents lived there for the rest of their lives, and they never returned to England.

My father loved his life in New Zealand. One day as we walked along the beach near their house he told me it was the best decision he could have made. But not long before she died, my mother said that if it had been up to her she would still be living in the house in Leicester that she had inherited from her parents. She never saw herself as a New Zealander, knew little about the country and its history, and when at the age of 62 I described myself as a New Zealander, she firmly told me that I was English!

As for me, although I was only nine when we came to New Zealand, even now I am aware that there are differences between me and my friends who were born here, and whose parents and grandparents were born here. Their childhood history is different to mine. Strangely, after all this time, I can still feel a bit of an outsider, as I did when I first came here as a child of nine.

I have been back to the UK twice. After the first visit in the 1960s when I lived in London for a year, I decided that indeed I was a New Zealander. I had gone there on an English passport, but next time I travelled I applied for New Zealand citizenship and a New Zealand passport.

I still feel strong links to England and to its history but I am very glad that my parents made the decision to come to New Zealand and that I grew up in this lovely place. I am proud to live here and to call myself a New Zealander.

I love to travel, perhaps a legacy from my childhood voyage half way round the world. In January this year I went to Costa Rica, a place I had always wanted to visit. It was when I was there that I realised the appeal of jungle and bright parrots was due to the time when as a child of nine, I stood on deck watching jungle-covered islands as the *Captain Cook* sailed through the Panama Canal.

Illustrations acknowledgement

All photographs and other original material were supplied by Carol Symington.

CHAPTER 6

Patricia Elsden

Name	Patricia Elsden
Ship	TSS *Captain Cook*
Departure date	10 December 1952
Arrival date	14 January 1953
Destination	North Island
Age	6

When I was six years old my parents left the UK to emigrate to New Zealand. At six, of course, I did not know the reason for the move. My only memory of knowing anything about New Zealand before we came was being told there were no snakes in New Zealand, a statement which turned out to be true. On the voyage out I was told it was the law in New Zealand that you must stay on one side of the pavement at all times, depending on which direction you were going in. This turned out to be not true!

On the trip out my mother and I shared a cabin (I think it was on B deck) with a Scotswoman, Jean Campbell, and her four-year-old daughter Margaret, who became our close friends for the trip. My father was relegated to D deck with the other husbands and single men. Jean's husband was in the army and already in New Zealand. Also in our six-berth cabin were a mother and her sullen teenage daughter who were most unfriendly to the rest of us. One night the mother insisted on having the porthole open even though the sea was quite rough. It was probably a blessing in a way, because according to my mother those two never had a bath during the whole trip! We woke to find the floor of the cabin awash, with our suitcases bobbing about, which didn't endear that woman to the other two.

My memory of the daily routine is very much associated with mealtimes; beef tea on deck for elevenses, high tea in the afternoons with yummy cakes, and lemonade and crisps in the saloon bars with our parents, who played a lot of cards. I was a very shy child and only formed a friendship with the little girl in our cabin. In spite of this I was never bored. My parents had a very social time, relaxing and drinking. For kids there were fancy-dress parties and the like. On Christmas Day we had a special meal with ice-cream, and every child received an orange and a stiff, shiny, commemorative hanky with a picture of the ship on it.

Patricia and her parents George and Betty Elsden on the TSS *Captain Cook*. Patricia is on the right, the girl on the left is Margaret Campbell who was in the cabin with Patricia's mother, also called Patricia. Margaret's father, like Patricia's father, was in the army.

One event that stuck in my mind was that a woman disappeared overboard one night. She was not recovered and my imagination went into overdrive.

En route, we had day stops in Panama and Curacao. I saw a monkey chained to a chair in Curacao, and a photo was taken of me and it. It was Christmas Eve in Panama City and there was a vast Christmas tree in the bank with a large number of broken glass baubles under it. We went back to the ship in a funny little colourful bus.

During the trip my parents seemed absolutely carefree; consequently so was I. Of course, I didn't realise it at the time, but for my parents it must have been absolutely thrilling after the stress and austerity of the war and post-war rationing. They were still young at 29 and 31, so having fun was still very important at that stage of their lives. They would have been worried about what was going to happen when we arrived in New Zealand, though, with very limited money.

I was feeling rotten as we approached New Zealand – as it turned out, I was coming down with measles by that time. When we first arrived in Wellington my mother looked down from her top bunk and said, "We're here, Patsy, in New Zealand." Then she gave a scream and nearly fell out of bed as she noticed I was absolutely smothered in measles. There had been an epidemic on board and I had escaped it until the very last day. I was taken to Wellington Fever Hospital along with lots of other sick children and spent about a week or ten days there. No visitors were allowed, nor were we able to have any toys or books with us.

This development threw everything into disarray, as my father, who had joined

Patricia and cabin mate Margaret in fancy dress.

the New Zealand army, had to report to Waiouru. So he just had time to take my mother by train up to Auckland to stay with our friends and former neighbours [from England, still friends today], then head back down there. At Taihape the train stopped for a rest break and my father rushed with everyone else to get tea. He kept trying to pay the cashier sixpence, which is what he thought she was repeatedly asking for. This was his first experience with the Kiwi accent; she was actually saying 'sivvenpince'!

In the hospital I was put in a large ward with all the other little 'orphans' and we all had to lie extremely still and be absolutely quiet. I don't think I spoke one word the whole time I was there; I was just petrified I would never see my parents again. My bowels didn't move once, so I was feeling very uncomfortable. We were fed and sponged in our beds, given bedpans and nobody got out of bed at all. The nurses would comb all our hair, one after another, with the same comb. (When I was finally reunited with my mother, she had the joy of discovering that I had head lice.) Once a day, in the afternoon, Matron would do a regal tour and if everything was neat and tidy and to her satisfaction, she would dole out one tiny dolly mixture sweetie each.

Finally the day came when we were to be allowed home, so we were taken to be bathed. We must have smelled really bad by then. The same bathwater was reused several times, much to my disgust. I have never forgotten that I had to get into the water after another small red haired boy stood up and blatantly wee'ed into the water. The nurse just added a splash of Dettol and told me to get in!

We were all taken to a kind of nursery-cum-waiting room with lots of books and toys. We had lunch and gradually the children were picked up by parents.

I was immersed in a book until it finally dawned on me that I was the only one left. Oh the pathos of it, but it's true – I remember feeling completely bereft and abandoned.

Eventually, quite late in the day, a nurse came for me, and there was a woman soldier waiting to take me away. Her name was Jean MacDonald and she was so kind to me. She was horrified that I had no clothes other than the pyjamas I was wearing, so she had the army driver stop in town so she could buy me a complete outfit, from underwear to ribbons for my (unknown to her) nitty plaits. It was almost closing time and we had to hurry to choose a dress and shoes and socks. This was all out of her own pocket and the goodness of her heart, and she sent a note with me to my mother next day, saying she wanted no reimbursement because she had enjoyed doing it. What an angel.

After I was all kitted out, we went to Fort Dorset, where I was to spend the night before I flew to Auckland the next morning. There were lots of lovely women there in the barracks. They all foraged around and found me little treats, like a toothbrush, a tiny tube of Colgate toothpaste, a little doll, a book and so on. I was quite overwhelmed by all that kindness.

Next morning, Jean took me in the staff car to the airport, and found a nice elderly lady to sit by me and keep an eye on me during the flight. I barely remember it as I was in a kind of frightened daze, but it must have taken a few hours to get from Wellington to Auckland in 1953, probably in some kind of Fokker Friendship. I remember the lady asking me who was meeting me, and me saying, "My mother is supposed to be, but she probably won't be there." Imagine my delight and relief, then, to find not only my mother waiting at Ardmore airfield, but also my best friend Diana, who had been my next door neighbour in England. I had missed her so much since her family had emigrated the year before. We were driven to Browns Bay in an army car and life slowly became more normal again. . . well, once the nits were dealt with!

After that my parents didn't ever look back. They seemed to find a social niche very quickly. We lived in Torbay and there were lots of parties, dances, amateur dramatics and so forth. We spent a lot of time at the beach, Browns Bay and Long Bay; absolute paradise. For me, of course, it was off to school and the usual childhood ups and downs. I did notice that ice-cream and lollies were much more readily available than they had been in England. (My mother still made me eat terrible food like oxtail soup, though.) I made friends with my parent's new friends' children.

I think my parents were a bit traumatised by our first Christmas in New Zealand (1953) when the chicken was cooked by a friend and it turned out to be full of maggots. We were living in very basic accommodation at the time with no proper oven and no fridge. We found it funny that we had to hang out a billy-can for milk, and the outside dunny was also a novel experience, especially the night soil man [whose job it was to take away the contents of the toilet can]. Ugh what a job!

We used to find that expression "night soil man" screamingly funny.

My parents must have missed their families and England at times, but I never once heard them say they wanted to go back.

As for me, I missed my grandparents and my cousin Michael. Eventually, in 1963, my maternal grandmother came out to join us. When I was in my late twenties, I left New Zealand to live in Australia, where I have lived ever since. Sometimes I wish we had not gone to the other side of the world, as I grew up rather lonely with no extended family. Also, as a result of all the sun exposure, I have an ongoing skin cancer problem. But all in all, and given the alternative of England at the time, it was no doubt the best thing all round.

Illustrations acknowledgement.

All photographs and other original material were supplied by Patricia Harper (nee Elsden).

CHAPTER 7

John and Doreen Hawkins

Name	John and Doreen Hawkins
Ship	TSS *Captain Cook*
Departure date	22 September 1953
Arrival date	1 November 1953
Destination	North Island
Marital status	Married
Profession	Farmers
Intention	To remain in New Zealand

John and Doreen Hawkins felt that the future of farming was not looking promising in Britain after the Second World War, so although they came from a close-knit family that they found difficult to leave behind, they were driven to seek a new country and a new lifestyle.

At the end of an unmemorable voyage out, the Hawkins disembarked and caught the overnight train from Wellington to Auckland.

Doreen recalls those first weeks in rural New Zealand.

Our first job after arriving in New Zealand was working on Milford Estate, a 3000 acre farm north of Auckland owned by three English men who provided us with a new two-bedroom cottage to live in. We worked normal hours, that is 8am to 5pm, unless it was shearing or mustering time, and our rate of pay was reasonable.

My impression was that rural New Zealand was a bit backward. On our arrival to our house we found a steamed pudding in a saucepan ready to heat up on the coal range – no electricity or telephone. We had no means of transport until the new Land Rover which we had sent out on another ship arrived three weeks after us, and there was nothing to do except meet a few neighbours.

We had borrowed furniture and we bought three new beds, dressing tables, dining table and chairs, and kitchen table and chairs, for four people.

England was still experiencing rationing when we left and New Zealand seemed to have plenty of normal food such as meat, butter and other items used daily.

We found variety was lacking, but we were already used to that due to the war years. The share-milker and family lived across the paddock from us, and we got free milk plus the use of their phone to order groceries from the dairy factory. We would ring our order through and the next morning it would be brought out by the cream truck to the cowshed. Once a day the school bus went to Wellsford and on its return trip it brought meat, bread and the mail. These were left in the mailbox or the children brought them in from the bus driver.

The first few weeks of our introduction to New Zealand was not so great.

We will never forget one tragic accident that happened shortly after we arrived. In the mornings our two children, our six-year-old son and eight-year-old daughter, went to the end of the farm entrance to catch the school bus to Wellsford Primary School. A little Maori boy also caught the school bus there. On the day of the tragedy the little Maori boy ran across the road and hid in some rushes. When he heard the cream truck arriving to collect the cream he ran out, thinking it was the school bus. He was killed in front of my children. Someone thought it was our son and went to tell John; it was a great relief to find out it wasn't our son but it was very tragic for the little boy's family. Our Land Rover was used to take the poor boy home. I attended the Tangi at Leigh, along with the schoolmaster.

Shortly after that tragedy, a young woman was drowned at Cara Beach, again in front of us, and again our Land Rover was used to transport the dead girl. Following that incident we sold the Land Rover and, using some sterling funds, bought a new Vauxhall car.

John and Doreen only stayed one year at Millbrook Estate after which time the owners dissolved the partnership that owned the farm. The Hawkins then moved to Bethlehem, Tauranga, with one of the former Millbrook Estate owners.

John and Doreen made return trips to Cornwall in England to visit parents and relatives and to see the homeland again, but they remained living in New Zealand and went on to have 15 grandchildren and seven great-grandchildren.

The hardships and trauma of resettling in another country were summed up by Doreen 55 years later: "Looking back I don't think I could do all this again."

CHAPTER 8

Dorothy Yates

Name	Dorothy Yates
Ship	TSS *Captain Cook*
Departure date	5 January 1954
Arrival date	11 February 1954
Destination	North Island
Marital status	Single
Profession	Qualified shorthand typist
Intention	To remain in New Zealand

My dissatisfaction with my job was ultimately what led me into immigrating to New Zealand. Although I was a qualified shorthand typist, working for the Midland bank in Reading, Berkshire, I only got to do that job when the manager's secretary was away. Instead I was a ledger operator almost all of the time. A case of "waiting to fill the dead man's shoes"; and it was boring. Consequently, I tended to browse the Situations Vacant columns for shorthand typists and that's when I saw a job with the words "see under New Zealand". When I read about the free passages to New Zealand, I applied.

In June I was interviewed at New Zealand House (or whatever it was called) [New Zealand Government Office, Pall Mall, London]. The gentleman was taking down my particulars and when he got to the "pastimes, hobbies", thinking of outdoor activities, I mentioned tennis. He then commented that it wasn't always hot and sunny, did I have any indoor hobbies. When I told him that I had done a lot of acting, he absolutely took off! It transpired he had been stage manager for Dunedin Operatic Society in New Zealand for some years and he talked on and on about their productions! There was no doubt that he approved of me! (When I arrived in New Zealand and was interviewed by the Chief at the Public Service Commission Head Office in Wellington, I could read – upside down – what he had said about me. Apparently, I was a "highly desirable" person to come to New Zealand!)

I knew practically nothing about New Zealand. However, I was at this time living in a YMCA hostel in Reading, and a New Zealand girl was living there. She told me that she felt sure that I was the right sort of girl to take the plunge, and would enjoy life in New Zealand. I did intend to stay in New Zealand, although if it had been awful I would either have remained for the two years of the bond and then gone home or, if I really couldn't stand it, I had enough money to repay my fare if necessary.

Both my parents had already died by the time I came to New Zealand, leaving me with one brother who was eight years older than I. Dad died in November 1946, when I was 18. My brother had not been long demobbed from the RAF. He had met his future wife, and as accommodation was in short supply after the war, he wanted to live with us after his marriage. We lived in Ripley, Derbyshire. Mum died in February 1950 when I was 21 and my brother's twin daughters were just five months old. Although the house was jointly owned, this left my brother and his family literally taking over the place, and certainly very little time and thoughts for me. So I moved away. My brother never bothered to keep in touch – all correspondence was on my side. (Yet I heard years later, from an aunt, that he cried when I came to New Zealand.)

The ship sailed from Glasgow. As I was going to Glasgow from Derbyshire, I went by train to Crewe, where I changed trains for Glasgow. In the waiting room at Crewe there was a girl from Wales, and as we looked for a sleeping car we found we were together. Another girl greeted us as we got on – Peggy Owen. We three chatted virtually the whole way north, all very excited. We stayed together, sharing the same table for our meals, along with three fellows going into the Air Force.

I also met Bill Kirby, an ex-Royal Marine Bandsman, who was returning to settle in New Zealand and take up farming. Bill later told me that he saw me at Glasgow railway station as we were to be taken on buses to the docks. Having already sailed to and from New Zealand six other times, he knew that having a friend to pass the time with was desirable (ha ha!), and decided I would do to pass the voyage with. Once we got on the ship he found a way to introduce himself, but it took a few days on voyage before I agreed to spending time in his company.

Bill was English and he'd been a musician in the Band of the Royal Marines, playing clarinet in the military band and violin in the orchestra band. My brother had learned to play the clarinet and saxophone whilst in the RAF, and I have a great love of music. We both love opera too. We'd hang over the side of the ship singing opera choruses etc. Five weeks can give you a good time to get to know one another.

On board the ship we were put into cabins in alphabetical order. With my surname being Yates, I ended up as the very last single person, and was in a four-berth cabin with three married women. Two of them had two sons each, and the husbands were together with the children in a six-berth cabin. When we first settled into our cabins we heard this announcement over the tannoy system: single men are not allowed in single women's cabins, and single women are not allowed in single men's cabins. Bill always reckoned he could come into mine because it was a married women's cabin! (He didn't!) The three married women soon got together to organise a timetable where one of them, plus spouse, could have time alone in the married men's cabin in the afternoon. I was pleased for them. It must have been hard for them separated in their voyage.

For the first four days on board we were left to find our way around. On the fifth day an Entertainments Committee was called for and I, along with another girl Edith, became joint secretaries. Each morning we would go to the Purser's office and help organise various activities. Although it was a smallish ship, with many passengers [about 1000], we had bingo each afternoon, whist, bridge, table tennis, chess, dances twice a week and cinema nightly. There were two sittings for meals, and the same "sittings" for the cinema. There were activities for the children. And we had a couple of fancy dress competitions, one for children, the other adults – the costumes that appeared on those occasions were quite incredible. Wonderful. I remember the first dance we had. We were crossing the Atlantic Ocean, mid winter, and the ship was pitching somewhat. We would trudge up the room one way, then skitter down the other side – quite an experience and lots of fun.

We were warned about overindulging with sunbathing, but some of the men on board were stupid – they got badly burned and were in sick bay for some time.

As Secretary of Entertainments, my life was full, office work in the morning, and helping with the other daily activities. The first few days, when the weather was good, I would sit outside on deck and do some embroidering I'd brought with me. Then I got busy! The day before we were due to land I started packing my cases, and suddenly thought – where is my embroidery? Nowhere to be seen. I spoke to the Purser. He said, "Come here, Dorothy" and opened two large drawers full of all manner of things. In one drawer was the embroidery, and the silks in the other. The amount of lost property was amazing: cameras etc, which many folk probably thought had been stolen – it was all there.

We had two stops on the trip, the first at Curacao. It was a Sunday and there was not a lot to do but it was good to have a look around. Then we went through the Panama Canal, with another few hours stop at Colon. By this time I was friendly with future husband Bill, and was well and truly chaperoned by him and one of the ship's officers. They took me to several nightclubs, but every time it was getting to a "revealing" part of the show they would whisk me away. Others came ashore later with lurid tales of what they'd seen. I'd seen nothing!

The trip to New Zealand was a wonderful experience, a very special trip and something which airplane travel can't compare with. Although sailing into the unknown we were well fed and cared for (the food better than in England, where we had still been rationed for many things). We knew there were jobs waiting for us, and accommodation. My life was secure, and I had a very happy and exciting time. I was never bored.

Because Bill had lived in New Zealand quite a lot since 1946 he had a considerable knowledge of the country. He also had an "adopted" New Zealand family with a Mum, six aunts and uncles and even a Grandma and Grandpa. And he was sure they would warmly welcome me. (They did.) He also had friends in Wellington, where I was heading.

I married Bill in 1955. We remained friends with Peggy (who also married a man she met on the ship, although that did not last.) We are Auntie and Uncle to her four children, and she to ours. We also stayed very friendly with another couple we met coming out, who have since died.

The evening we arrived in Wellington Harbour the Immigration Officials came on board and gave us our instructions. Next day there was a bus to take several of us (all girls) to Trentham Immigration Camp. There we were greeted, told to get ourselves into pairs, and we were taken to our rooms in Nissan Huts. There would have been about 12 of us. My roommate was a teacher going to Taita School. All the other girls had become friendly on that ship with the RAF chaps, who were in Wellington waiting for the 8pm ferry to Lyttelton, and they [the girls] all caught the next train into Wellington, leaving me on my own.

I explored the camp while everyone else was at work. I found a communal lounge, with a radio which I turned on – the programme "Gems from the Operas" was announced. Great, I thought. Gigli sang "Your Tiny Hand is Frozen" from La Boheme … and then came the song: "If you love the sizzle of a sausage, the sausage is a Swan – there's nothing finer when the sausage is a Swan"! I was gobsmacked! I'd never heard radio advertisements before. England didn't have them at the time. We then had another lovely aria followed by Sausages again. I have never forgotten that.

The following morning (Friday), we were taken into Wellington, and I met my boss and the rest of the staff at the Head Office of the Public Service Commission. I was then told to go and have a look at Wellington and to return there on Monday morning at 8am. It was there that I worked for the next three months.

For the first six weeks I lived at the Immigration Hostel. However, this meant rising at 6am each weekday, to have breakfast and be at the railway station to catch the 6.45am train into Wellington. This arrived at 7.45am, leaving just time to walk to the office in Bowen Street. I left work at 4.40pm to catch the 5pm train back to Trentham, arriving an hour later, so back home at 6.15pm. It made a long day. After six weeks we saw an advert for a house to rent for several months, belonging to a family in Lower Hutt who were going abroad for a year, and four of us shared the renting. This cut my travelling time by well over half.

We four girls got along fine. All of us had developed other friendships – mine was of course Bill, now in Taranaki. I went up there for the Easter break, and met his special New Zealand family. It was then that I decided to move to Taranaki so we could be together.

Under the New Zealand Immigration Scheme all immigrants must remain in New Zealand for two years, or repay their fares. As long as one remained in one's designated profession one could work anywhere in the country … except if one were a shorthand typist, when the Public Service kept a rigid hold on you. As regards myself, I had to have the Banns already being read before I could move to Taranaki.

I was not going to marry unless we had more time to know one another without being in holiday mode. So I came up to New Plymouth and within a day was offered the position of Secretary to the General Manager of the Farmers Cooperative of New Zealand (now Taranaki Farmers), which I accepted and started work there a week later. He offered me the same salary, so without any travelling expenses I was considerably better off, despite paying the £5 a month for breaking my contract. Working in New Zealand compared with the bank in England was much more relaxed. I'd been used to calling my superiors "Sir", or at least "Mr. ...", and the first thing I was told was "no mister – I'm Fred". It took a bit of getting used to.

My fiancé Bill was employed on a farm near Eltham by this time, a stud farm, and the owners invited me to their home every single weekend – a wonderful opportunity for this townie to learn to milk cows, etc. Because I had walked out of my job in Wellington I paid £20 of my £86 fare back, and negotiated to pay £5 each month to the Labour Department in New Plymouth. After a few months they asked me why and what was it for. When I told them they commented that they were so short of shorthand typists I would have been welcomed by them. But of course, Public Service had refused to move me, and had cut off their nose to spite their face!

One day one of the senior staff asked me if I was still paying back my fare. On hearing that I was he told his friend Mr Aderman, MP for New Plymouth, who asked to see me. He then brought up my case in Caucus, and I received a letter to say that the remainder of my fare was being wiped. That £30 bought our dining suite! At that talk with Mr Aderman I had said that several people had worked their two years, then gone back to Britain, no use to the country. But I was going to be a farmer's wife and work the rest of my life for the country, and I felt it most unfair.

When I came to Taranaki mid-May, I was able to temporarily live with friends of Bill's in New Plymouth. After a couple of weeks there was a vacancy at the YMCA Residential Hostel there, so I moved in. It was only 100 yards from my office, wonderfully close. When living in Reading, Berkshire, I had resided at a YMCA hostel – and the difference was considerable! Of course we had still been partially rationed in England, and that naturally made a difference. However, in New Plymouth there were tablecloths, cloth table napkins, bowls of whipped cream to add to one's desserts, and choices of meals – like being in a hotel. And when I left to be married a year later they put on a mock wedding dinner for me, the tables set round in a horseshoe and every one of the girls gave me something at my surprise gift evening. Such a wonderful surprise – so kind of them all.

Because some rationing was still in force when I lived in England, there wasn't much I missed in the way of food. I remember my first meal in New Zealand, at Trentham Immigration Hostel. There were huge trays of sliced roast mutton, plus trays of roast vegetables etc – you just helped yourself to as much as you wished. New Zealand really did seem to be the land of plenty.

Some sweets had different names. I went into a shop and asked for "a quarter of bulls' eyes", and was just stared at. Evidently it was "four ounces of black balls". Maltesers were a sweet I missed – and in England they were never called lollies!

I was pleased I had brought some good quality clothing with me. I had stocked up, before leaving, and was glad I did. Clothing was much dearer here, and shoes too. As I eventually was a farmer's wife, my good clothes lasted me a while, and when eventually I needed more I found it far easier to make my own. I must admit that the dress materials for sale here, the variety, was much better than in most places in England.

In England I had been used to enjoying an evening socialising in a pub – and found that ladies didn't go into them in New Zealand. Anyway, they closed at 6pm, after the so-called 5 o'clock pig swill! I was aware of the men leaving work at 4.40 to 5pm, and drinking as much as they could, on an empty stomach, before being turned out, quite intoxicated at 6pm. I well remember seeing bottles of beer, having slipped from drunken hands as they went up the steps into Wellington railway station, lying smashed on the steps. My friend called it "having one for the road"!

In Wellington in 1954 there was a New Settlers Club, where dances were held, and not only British immigrants gathered, but other nationalities too. I went there a few times before leaving for Taranaki. I also attended a Baptist Church in Lower Hutt, and found good friends there. Bill had friends in Khandallah, and the two boys in the family took me on their motorbikes, and showed me around the area. When I lived in New Plymouth Bill was working on a farm outside Eltham. The day I got my job there we bought a Ford Prefect car. It was obvious a car was essential in our lives. My parents had never had one – there was a bus in any

Walk-through milking shed.

Photo courtesy of Phyllis Young

Photo courtesy of Phyllis Young

In the milk shed. Milk going into cans.

Photo courtesy of Phyllis Young

Stand for the milk and cream to go on the truck to the dairy factory.

direction from my hometown, every 15 minutes, so no need at all. But here, oh yes, most necessary. After just a week or two, Bill's boss invited me to the farm for the weekend … then the next weekend … and so on. I learned what cows look like, and how to milk them. We played tennis at the local club and enjoyed the dances at the local country hall (later playing indoor bowls and table tennis there in the winter time).

Having lived close to London for a few years, and taken advantage of the special price for trains there for an evening, I had enjoyed many trips to shows for the cost of 10/- (= $1.00) for train and theatre. Here there was only the cinema, and I noticed that folk booked and went to the cinema in New Zealand, dressed as they would for a theatre evening in England. But my philosophy was – you don't live your life on the stage or the dance floor. Other things are far more important. Not long after I was married I joined an amateur theatre company and enjoyed several years of involvement with them, until twin babies made those activities a bit too much.

So on 14 May 1955 Bill and I were married and have been together ever since. Good years. No regrets. We dairy farmed, though didn't manage to own our own place. We sharemilked. Never a big farm like they have today, and always milked in a walk-through shed – never even managed a herringbone shed, let alone a rotary milking shed. Milking took a long time that way but we managed.

We adopted two children, as following an appendix operation in England when I was 18, with adhesions on the fallopian tubes, I was told never to expect any children. But at 40 I gave birth to a twin son and daughter who celebrated their 40th birthday in July 2008. A shock at the time, but oh, the great pleasure we have had from them all.

It has been a busy and a happy life. In 1955 I joined the Women's Institute, then I had two years with Women's Division of Federated Farmers followed by 15 more with Women's Institute. Then, since 1973, I've been with Women's Division of Federated Farmers [now Rural Women New Zealand], the past 22 years as Stratford's Secretary, plus Treasurer since October 2001.

I honestly feel that I've experienced a far better and happier life than I would have done had I remained in England. And the more I see on TV, and read of life in Britain these days, the more both Bill and I are pleased that we both came and settled here. There may be no blood relations around, but the friendships we have made over these years have been quite wonderful.

CHAPTER 9

Dorothy Horne

Name	Dorothy Geraldine Horne
Ship	TSS *Captain Cook*
Departure date	13 April 1954
Arrival date	19 May 1954 (disembarked 20 May 1954)
Destination	South Island
Martial status	Single
Profession	SRN (State Registered Nurse)
Intention	To return to England in two years

Barnsley nurse is to sail for New Zealand

NURSE DOROTHY HORNE, who has been 12 months at Barnsley Beckett Hospital, daughter of Mr. and Mrs. E. Horne, of 203, Park-road, Barnsley, is emigrating to New Zealand.

Nurse Horne

She finished work at Beckett Hospital this week and sails a week on Tuesday from Glasgow.

Aged 24, she has been nursing since she left school. When 17 years old, and at Barnsley High School, she half considered staying on to become a teacher, but finally decided to enter nursing.

She spent 12 months in a Mansfield hospital, then over three years in London, including a long spell at the Royal Canadian Hospital, and gained her S.R.N. She also has midwifery and orthopaedic qualifications.

Her mother said this week: "She has always had this urge to travel. She thought about America and Canada, but finally settled for New Zealand. There is a position waiting for her there."

Said her father (a printer in Barnsley): "They say New Zealand is very much like England. She should do well there."

Courtesy Barnsley Chronicle. April 1954

Wording on badge: "Canadian Red Cross Memorial Hospital."

Wording on badge: "The General Nursing Council For England & Wales."

The Canadian Red Cross Memorial Hospital, Taplow, Maidenhead, Berks, England.

Becketts Hospital 1953. Dorothy was a Staff Nurse in 1953 and saving up to buy her SRN (State Registered Nurse) belt. Nurses had to buy the belts themselves. The pinafores worn in this photo were not allowed to be worn off the Ward. Dorothy is at the very front on the left.

This chapter is comprised of correspondence from Dorothy Geraldine Horne to her parents back in Barnsley, England. The first communication they would have received was a postcard dated 13 April 1954. The next "letter" would have been six aerograms posted from Caracas 29 April 1954 at a cost of 6d each. The second "letter" they would have received was written between 3 May and 17 May 1954 and consisted of 17 pages of A4 airmail-weight paper. The rest of the letters were written from the Burwood Hospital in Christchurch New Zealand between 4 June and 4 August 1954.

Front and back of the postcard dated 13 April 1954 that Dorothy sent to her parents back in England.

[No. 1 Aerogram, dated 19 April 1954, postmarked Curacao and written on the TSS *Captain Cook*.]

My Dear Mum and Dad,

Really there's so much to say I don't know where to begin. We have just had a small storm but nothing of any consequence. Well, to start with, I haven't been seasick. Lots have and still are, but you can now tell everyone that I am a good sailor. The weather has brightened up again; we're coming into the tropics now so it's rather warm!

The meals are really good, you'll be pleased to hear, and I am acquiring a nice fat bottom sitting around all day.

There are two nurses in the cabin with me! It's a six berth cabin and very nice indeed – I have a top bunk, but have learned to climb into it without using the ladder!

The baths are salt water, but to tell the truth, apart from the fact that it's impossible to get any lather from the soap, I find it very refreshing. We have special sea water soap, but it's not very successful.

The ship really is just the job Mum and Dad; you needn't worry about any lack of comfort in that direction anyway.

I am on the concert committee you'll be interested to hear! We have to give a big concert at the end of the voyage and a small sort of concert entertainment each

Dorothy in the yellow sweater and cap.

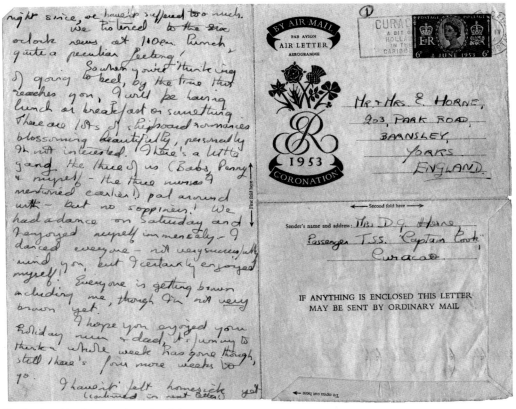

The front and back pages of number 1 Aerogram.

week. There's a really mixed lot on board the ship – all trades and professions and lots of nurses. It's funny how soon we have all got to know each other. You know my little yellow cap? Well, it's really hitting it off with the crew. I'm told that the first engineer wants it and various members of the crew have made cracks about it! The yellow sweater has been extremely handy too.

You know, I'm glad I bought the things I did, in fact I'm beginning to wish I had bought more shoes. Cigarettes are ever so cheap, Daddy dear – even you would smoke if you were here, just for the thrill of being able to smoke cheaply!

We are wakened at 6.30am with a cup of tea, but as the clocks have been going back every night, an hour the first two nights and half an hour every night since, we haven't suffered too much.

We listened to the six o'clock news at 1pm lunch, quite a peculiar feeling!

So when you're thinking of going to bed, by the time this reaches you, I will be having lunch or breakfast or something. There are lots of shipboard romances blossoming beautifully; personally I'm not interested. There's a little gang the three of us (Babs, Penny and myself – the three nurses I mentioned earlier!) pal around with – but no soppiness! We had a dance on Saturday and I enjoyed myself immensely – I danced every one – not very successfully mind you, but I certainly enjoyed myself! Everyone is getting brown including me, though I'm not very brown yet.

I hope you enjoyed your holiday Mum and Dad, It's funny to think a whole week has gone though, still here's for more weeks to go.

I haven't felt homesick yet.

[Continued on No. 2 Aerogram, postmarked Curacao and written on the TSS *Captain Cook*.]

As I said, I haven't felt homesick as yet, probably because we are so completely all off in a little world of our own, that it just doesn't sink in! I don't know what will happen when I receive (if I receive) your letters at Curacao. Anyway, we're only there for thirty-six hours.

There are 300 children on this boat, and I pity their parents, the things they get up to; good job you didn't decide to emigrate with us when we were kids. Anyway you would have been seasick Mum, there's no way of getting away from the "up and down and roundabout" motion of the ship.

I am now learning to call various parts of the ship by their proper names, I've stopped calling port-holes "windows" and blithely talk about the port and starboard sides, and I've stopped going up and down into forsaken places looking for our cabin!

The present captain is a new one, Captain Cook himself retired last voyage and as far as we can gather it's a good job. I'm told that he didn't bother much about the passengers and that on the last voyage he went out of the Clyde in the midst of a soaring gale thereby reducing a third of the passengers to prostrate messes, whereas this captain carefully plans the route to avoid rough seas! It's a strange sensation to look out in all directions and see nothing but moving masses of water! Babs, Penny and I take a mile walk around the deck every morning. Don't think that means the ship is a mile long, we merely walk round and round the promenade deck 17½ times. Before breakfast too! Despite that, I think I am putting on weight! I have taken several snaps, but I'm really waiting for the hot weather when I can wear my shorts and sun top!

Give my love to everybody won't you Mum and Dad. I will write again later on.

[Tuesday 20 April]

They are having PT at 7am every day and very enthusiastically the three of us were going to attend. However, as this morning came around the enthusiasm was somewhat dampened, particularly as it was raining! Somebody once told me it didn't rain at sea, not in the usual manner anyway, just storms – anyway it's not true, it drizzles just the same!

There are three Master at Arms on board this ship, and their special function is to chase recalcitrant "love birds" off the decks at 11pm. One of the girls in our cabin, a Lancashire girl called Alice, has become well acquainted with the Master at Arms as a result! Even I have been chased away on one occasion when I was talking to some members of the crew!

[Continued on No. 3 Aerogram, postmarked Curacao and written on the TSS *Captain Cook*.]

The ship's doctor gave us a little pep talk yesterday about what not to do when we get to the tropics. We aren't to go out in the sun for more than five minutes a day, we have to take extra salt and try and drink more fluids! Although it's very warm, we haven't really seen any tropical sun yet. I hope it doesn't rain at Curacao!

We held a talent competition last night to try and find people for our concert – there seems to be a lot of potential Frankie Lanes and Johnny Rays amongst the passengers.

I have just laddered one of my nylons, to my annoyance! Anyway nylons are sold on the ship and very nice ones too, 1/- a pair!

I wish you were here with me, it would be a grand holiday for you, except that Dad would morally be frustrated at not having anything much to do! Mind you there's quite a decent programme of entertainment worked out, and we have two films a week, and two dances – not "old time" though!

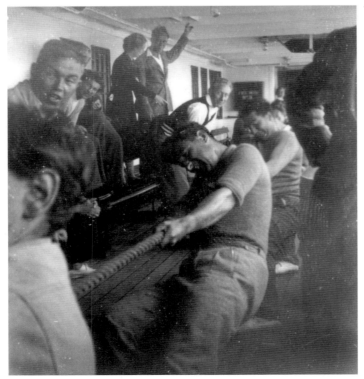

Tug-of-war on deck.

Venezuelan schooners with fruits, Curacao.

[No. 4 Aerogram, dated 24 April 1954, postmarked Curacao and written on the TSS *Captain Cook*.]

Dear Mum and Dad,

I have just made a mistake and put a letter in the box for you which is not yet sealed so whether or not you will receive it I don't know – anyway I'll continue on here! You will have to pass round this last letter Mum because I wrote to the others a few days ago and I'm telling you things I haven't told them!

To start with, HEAT! I'm sweltering here I can tell you. Never, no, never, have I been so hot. Yesterday, I sat in the sun for one hour and burnt my shoulder, so you can guess how hot it is!

Now for the great news! Yesterday, six of us went for TEA WITH THE CAPTAIN! Penny and I and four other nurses were amongst the lucky ones and were thrilled to bits as you can guess! We had a very pleasant afternoon, the Captain cracked a few jokes and we obediently laughed! We also had two cakes each and as we only have horrid little buns for tea in the dining rooms we appreciated the difference. Also on Tuesday, the same six of us had tea with the NZ liaison officer and his wife, so we are now walking around with swollen heads!

The ship is in the blue Caribbean Sea now, the happy hunting grounds of Captain Morgan in the bad old days! It is blue too, which is more frustrating when we are all sitting around with sweat falling off us in great beads!

The children are very fretful these days too, poor little things!

Oh by the way Mum – I'm pleased to see that Brooke beat Bishop Auckland after all – there you will wonder how I know that. Well there is a daily news sheet put up on the notice board and it was there I read it!

We arrive in Curacao tomorrow afternoon and what I'm looking forward to, is buying some fruit. Pineapples, melons and etcetera we can get there, I am told – oh boy!

The time in England is now 2.30pm – here it is only 9.30am – funny isn't it?

We had a film again last night, you have no idea how pleasant it is to sit out in the cool night air and watch a film!

I have seen lots of flying fish now – shoals of them all seem to rise from the water at the same time and go skimming across the water. We haven't had anything more exciting than that as yet, but here's hoping! We sighted an island on the starboard side of the ship this morning – it looked like this.

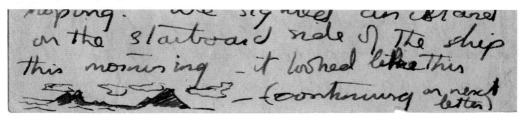

Dorothy's sketch of the first sighting of the island.

The land in the left of the photo is the same as in the sketch.

Photo courtesy of Phyllis Young

Dorothy has written on the back: "Some of the RNZAF lads on the for'ard deck."

[Continued on No. 5 Aerogram, postmarked Curacao and written on the TSS *Captain Cook*.]

Don't forget to pass this letter round will you Mum and Dad? The weather is much too hot to write a lot of letters! Anyway they have to be posted by 12 midday. We aren't at the equator yet either, so what will happen when we arrive there – goodness only knows!

Do you remember that little paper fan I had? Well I don't know why I brought it, I'm sure, but I'm fully thankful I did – it's coming in very handy I can tell you!

A good job I bought those shorts too Mum, and that shirt, I wear them most of the time!

People are wearing their briefest of brief attire, all the men displaying hairy legs and knobbly knees. It's difficult to try and imagine what the weather must be like at home now, is it cold or warm – whatever it is like it couldn't be as hot as here!

Oh well Mum and Dad I think I have told you everything that has happened so far and I had better write a note to Aunty Dolly and Uncle Ted – give my love to Mr and Mrs Sykes and Mr and Mrs Barnes etc. I'll drop them a postcard, but as it won't arrive for a week or two, just tell them I haven't forgotten them!

Bless you.

Love Dorothy G.

I have written an extra bit in the back for Roy, Alan and their ladies!

Dear Roy, Alan, Inez and Beryl,

Just an extra bit to share between you. You would be mighty jealous if you could see my tan, my shoulder is a bit sore mind you, otherwise I'm turning a lovely golden brown. Cripes though, I've always boasted I never perspired (huh!) but by golly, there are drops on my fevered brow right now!

Anyway kids, love to you all – and a hot sticky kiss for my little Chris.

Love,

Dorothy G.

[No. 6 Aerogram, dated 27 April 1954, postmarked Cristobal, Canal Zone and written on the TSS *Captain Cook*.]

My dear Mum and Dad,

I haven't time to write a long letter this time, and anyway you did pretty well out of the last lot, so I'll just tell you about Curacao!

To start with, the whole place reeks of oil – its sole industry is oil refinery. Mind you it isn't a dirty place by any means, and if you could see the houses painted all colours with large Venetian blinds and shutters, and no glass in – just like dolls houses! The population is mainly Negro and they are all beautifully clean and dressed. The shops are full of export stuff from England and you'd be surprised if you could see some of the things we produce and never see. Everyone seems to have a car, and huge American ones at that, and they go tearing along the narrow roads at ridiculous speeds. I took a lot of snaps on the way in, and some day when I get them all developed you shall have some!

When we finally docked, everyone tore off the ship like mad things, to be greeted by a small shower – anyway that didn't last long and we set off to have a look round. The shops of course were all shut, which was rather fortunate – everything is very dear, something to do with devaluation of the £1. The seamen's mission was open and we were able to buy things from there, but even then I couldn't afford much! I bought a scarf and a little pin cushion dog!

The first thing we did when we left the ship was to go to the swimming pool – and we thoroughly enjoyed ourselves there – except that the water in the pool is drawn from the sea and as the sea for miles around is covered with oil the water didn't taste very nice! Anyway, it was worth it!

There was a terrific to-do on the docks about 11pm – fortunately or otherwise I was in bed (or bunk). I didn't see a thing – but it transpires that a lot of the Negroes tried to interfere with some of the girls from the ship, and the crew, most of whom were drunk as lords, started a terrific fight in front of the ship. Knives, razors – everything came out. There were a lot of injuries, but no-one was killed! Mind you, don't blame the Negroes – a lot of the crew started the trouble by going round the town picking quarrels with the Negroes – so really it was half a dozen of one and six of the other!

Leaving Curacao.

As a result of all this we were jolly glad to get away from Curacao. Not a place I would choose to live in I think. The heat is really terrific nowadays – everything goes sticky, including ourselves! I've never been so hot anyway!

Tomorrow we arrive in Panama – much better I believe! We all go ashore in gangs so you needn't worry. I wouldn't dream of wandering around these places alone or just with girls – it just isn't safe – but I never realised just how unsafe until Curacao!

I'm glad you enjoyed your holiday Ma and Pa. I doubt whether you would if you'd had weather like we're having now! There have been two appendectomies on board poor things! Not the sort of weather for that sort of thing. Thanks for the long letter, Dad, yes I did manage to read it – with a microscope mind you! For the moment – adieu.

Love

Your daughter.

[Letter dated 3 May 1954, written on the TSS *Captain Cook*.]

My Dear Mum and Dad and Family,

To save constant repetition I am going to make this a combined letter to pass around! Okay, lazy me! I know! Anyway, it will be a long one because I have so many things to tell you all!

Let's start with Cristobal and the Panama! We arrived in Cristobal, which is the part at the beginning of the Panama Canal. You know all the pictures one sees of

Dorothy's illustration of the straw hat she bought in Cristobal. She has written: "Slightly exaggerated but you'll get the general idea!"

tropical parts – houses above ground level – palm trees – banana trees – drinking places with swing doors – the LOT! Well, that's Cristobal. I went ashore to a party and enjoyed myself thoroughly. We drank coffee, pineapple, pear juice, tomato juice, ate enormous steak sandwiches the size of one meal and generally wandered around like gullible British travellers! Things were very cheap in comparison with English prices, but we were cheated by Panama standards! I bought a lovely sandalwood fan – hand painted, a large silk stole and a straw hat with a huge brim! We had an afternoon and an evening there. It was, of course, very hot but we didn't mind that so much, everything was so exciting!

A mule at the Pedro Miguel Locks, Panama Canal.

We also bought lots of fruit, bananas etc including a huge melon. The prices – well, your mouths'd water if I told you!

The next day we came through the Canal proper and we sat on the for'ard deck all day and watched the whole process! First of all we passed through several locks, the first few lifted the ship up and the end ones lowered us down. You would have been amazed the way everything worked – just like clockwork. There were cute little engines called "mules" which pulled us into the locks.

In the middle of the canal there are one or two lakes – fresh water lakes at that, and everyone made a quick dash for the baths in order to have a real freshwater bath!

We looked hard along the banks for alligators but to my acute disappointment, not one showed up its ugly snout the whole way! Don't imagine the banks are desert – that's very far from the truth – in actual fact miles of JUNGLE – the real thing stretches on either side. All very strange and exciting. The whole distance took about eight hours. Now, we are in the Pacific. Home waters to us New Zealanders! The last couple of days have been as unlike tropical weather as you can imagine – the wind is strong and rather cool but when it drops, or out in the sun, it's really very warm indeed. People have found themselves peeling and blistering without recalling how it happened. Me? Well I'm not doing any of those things – I've turned brown and I am staying that way – so far anyway!

Yesterday we passed over the Equator, but we didn't have a big ceremony because so many of the passengers on this ship have never been over the Equator, that it would have taken all day! Anyway I have a certificate as a souvenir, though I must admit I feel a little cheated!

If you could all see me now, you'd have pink fits. Legs eleven and all that. You have no idea how useful this little outfit Aunty Annie gave me has been. The sun

Fresh water lakes in the middle of the Panama Canal.

Photo courtesy of Phyllis Young

Dorothy has written on the back: "A view along the Panama Canal. From the for'ard deck. TSS *Captain Cook*."

top part is rather more than a little daring, but no one seems to mind what they wear, so I've stopped bothering too!

Two days ago we felt a bump – the whole ship shook – and would you believe it – a whale had foolishly placed itself in the way of the prow and we had run into it. That of course brought the sharks on the scene – scent of blood and all that – a messy business!

We should really be very thankful for the winds I suppose, because at least we don't feel the heat as much as we have done and – believe me – that really is a welcome relief. I have never been as hot in my life as we were coming across the Caribbean Sea and through the Panama.

This afternoon we are commencing rehearsals for the concert we give at the end of the voyage – I believe I mentioned I am on the committee. Gives me something to do anyway! I'm afraid I occasionally get rather bored with having nothing to do!

[Continued on 5 May 1954]

Well Mum, Dad and everybody,

Three more days have passed without anything exciting happening – apart from the fact that I, ME, am going in for the "Miss Captain Cook" competition. I'm terrified – anyway I haven't a hope as you will realize – anyway, must play the game and all that! Somebody put my name down for it and what with one thing and another I agreed – I will probably have to be carried off in a dead faint!

We ate our last pineapple and coconut yesterday – today we start on the bananas and then we must look forward to two fruitless weeks! If you look on the map you will see that this part of the journey is the longest stretch of landless water there is – and as a consequence the water is rationed – drinking water, that is. The taps are turned on for so many hours a day – and you know how I liked drinking water – well, you can believe me, I'd give a month's pay for a drink of real lovely cool water! Nothing else but ordinary common old garden H_2O. Lovely!

Oh dear – I keep thinking about this competition – my knees are knocking. Anyway, there's a knobbly knees competition for the men that should be interesting! We also have a fancy dress dance this weekend and I'm borrowing a rugby outfit from one of the boys – not very original but it will do!

You will all be very interested to hear that on this boat there is a very nice young man by the name of Alan Cook, a sheep farmer by profession, and he's really rather nice! He looks like our Alan funnily enough! There now, no further comment!

The weather is still very hot, but there is still a pretty stiff wind, so outside at least it's fairly cool!

A very amusing feature of this ship is the "Courting Couple Group". It's great fun to walk around the boat deck about 10.45pm and watch them all hard at work! The poor Master at Arms whose job it is to clear the deck at 11pm walks around with his eyes averted, flashing his torch in the most secret nooks and crannies! You'd be amazed where people manage to cram themselves!

The time here is 10pm – the time for you is 5pm – we'll soon be living in different days – next Tuesday we cross the date line and we go to bed on Tuesday night and wake up Tuesday morning!

[Continued on Sunday 9 May 1954, 9am]

A few more days and we will be in Wellington – ten days to be precise! Today, the weather is not so good – the sea is very choppy and the boat is rolling around like a barrel. Lots of people are seasick again, but I can report, with pleasure, that up to the moment I am still feeling fit and hearty!

We had the Fancy Dress Parade last night, and some of the costumes were really good! As reported earlier I went in a rugby outfit! Complete with the "pill" – I believe, that's the name! No I didn't win a prize! Alan went as Mr Corville the liaison officer – very good too, and won a prize amongst the most original! I was called out amongst the best dressed but that was as far as it went.

You know I said I was going in for the "Miss Captain Cook" parade – well, I found out at the last minute that I wasn't allowed to enter being a member of the committee (the concert committee, you remember!). You can imagine I was pleased, to say the least.

There's really nothing of great interest to report about the last few days. We have merely ate, slept and sun bathed – a thoroughly lazy time all round. I can't see myself working somehow! Think I might marry a millionaire or something and live a life of luxury! As we approach NZ everyone is feverishly swotting up all they can about conditions and living there. We are being shown films about the country – in fact, full scale propaganda!

From the windows of the lounge the seas come up to meet us, then down we go and we see all sky – very upsetting for a delicate stomach – anyway Mum, you can't say I have a delicate stomach now can you? Well, I think that's the little lot for today! More later!

[Continued on 12 May 1954]

Rugby fancy dress.

Nearer and nearer. We are all beginning to feel that the end really is in sight. I feel thrilled, excited, apprehensive, etcetera and etcetera! In less than a fortnight now your daughter will be running around making beds, dressing wounds (oh no – come to think of it, I might be patting baby's backs and changing nappies!), in fact, back to WORK! Well, I won't be sorry; I've had a good holiday!

We are in the processes of the ship's concert, I will enclose a programme with the letter – I am in the sketch entitled "Nifty Nana and Pickpocket Sam".

The films we are being shown now are documentaries of New Zealand. I wish you could see them Mum, Dad, Roy, Alan, Beryl and Inez – you would be writing to the emigration office pronto, I must say, the country certainly looks beautiful – in fact if it's only half as good as it looks, it's really good! Anyway, I will be relating all the ins and outs of NZ during the next two years at least, so you will be hearing more about it from first hand experience.

The weather hasn't been so good since we passed the Pitcairn Islands (look that up on the map!), but all the same I've managed to retain a smashing brown! Every day, we compare arms on our table and I'm holding my own quite nicely!

On Saturday there is the farewell dinner and dance – I believe it is customary for everyone to hit the high spots. Anyway, we have ordered two bottles of Sauterne (white wine in case you didn't know!) for the eight of us on our table – all females incidentally, but we will, of course, join our respective group of men after the dinner! I have a little collection to myself – Alan Cook included – but as you will gather he's the one I like best!

This letter is going to be quite expensive as far as weight's concerned despite the fine paper. Gee Dad, I'm fully thankful for the writing pad you gave me!

Concert Programme for the final concert: "CAPTAIN COOK-OOS" CONCERT PARTY presents Talent That CAPTAIN COOK DIDN'T DISCOVER.

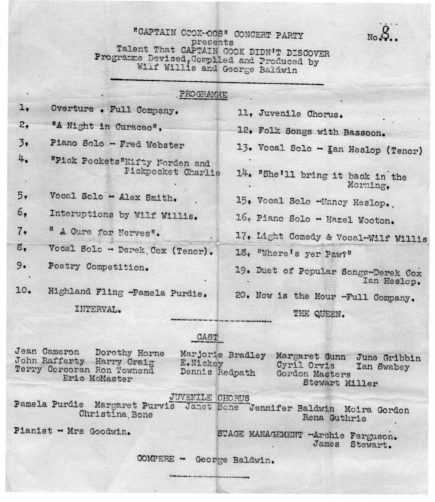

We are all discarding summer clothes etcetera now the weather is much cooler, and frankly I'm not sorry!

By the way, I misinformed you about the date line. What actually happens, is, that there will be no Tuesday for us next week. We jump straight from Monday to Wednesday! Okay!

[Continued on 13 May 1954]

My dear family, everything is, as before, another lazy day! I have had the misfortune to acquire an attack of gastritis but don't alarm yourselves, half the ship has had it – we think it's possibly due to the water or something like that. As a tank empties the water gets very brown and rusty looking! Anyway, I'm not suffering severely or anything, it's just a feeling of discomfort – colic you know?

Some of the "gang" relaxing on the deck.

Tonight we give the last performance of our concert, and the Captain and officers will be there! I think I'll go off sick!

All around me are lolling figures reading, chatting and generally relaxing in complete abandon!

It's funny though, I can't concentrate on books – you're right, I am an old shuffle bottom! Alas I think I have fallen hook, line and sinker for A.C. (look back!) aren't I fickle – I really feel ashamed of myself, poor Vash, I hope he's recovered okay. Well, never mind, lots of fun and all that! See, that's what happens when you go for a cruise. However, when I return to work all this will remain in my memory as a pleasant and unusual experience!

I am at present wearing my yellow sweater, I wear it all the time now that the weather has changed. Honestly, I just wouldn't have been given a more useful and "happy" present.

As I write this you will be (or should be!) snoring away in bed – it's about midnight to you and 2.30 approx pm for us – can you imagine the differences in time in relation to me? I find it difficult I must say! Somehow, I can't get over the feeling that it's all a dream and you'll be waiting to greet me off the boat and that I will go back to the Beckett Hospital and WORK! The work part of it still applies, of course, but it won't be Becketts, will it?

The yellow sweater.

I have actually collected all sorts of odds and sods and will eventually sort them out and send you various souvenirs etc – photographs and the like. At the moment, anyway, it's impossible, so don't get impatient and think I've forgotten!

Gee! I hope you can read this letter.

[Continued on Saturday 15 May 1954]

Yesterday we had the worst storm we have had so far, not that it wasn't fine or anything, but a terrific gale was (and still is, for that matter!) blowing and the ship was, and is, rocking all the way round the clock. Actually, I must say I rather enjoy the little storms at sea, they certainly make the voyage more interesting, though it's not a thing I love to say out loud because I would be very unpopular with the set of people who suffer every time it's rough! My stomach, by the way, troubles me no longer; I have completely recovered from the little upset previously mentioned! Only three or four more days and then we will know!

Tonight we are having the farewell dinner, and I believe I will probably be "tipsy", it's the custom anyway, and I wouldn't like to be an odd one out.

Well Mum and Dad and family, I think I will make this letter – I mean today's epistle, the end. I will of course write about Wellington and everything when I finally arrive at my unknown destination!

I hope this has given you some idea about what's been happening to me and so on and will bring a little piece of me back to you. I love you all very much you know, bless you! Don't worry about me, I'm going to be all right, I have the family ability to get on well with people if I wish (sounds conceited doesn't it, but you know what I mean!), so I will be okay!

Whatever you do don't WORRY about me. I will have my moods, you all know them well, but you know it's up hill and down dale with me.

Goodbye – my very dear family for the moment! I have a picture of you all in my mind which will be a big light wherever I go. No girl ever had a better family and a better start in life.

Your loving Daughter,

Sister &

Aunty.

Dorothy G.

P.S. Reading through this letter, there are one or two things I could mention! Did I tell you about life-boat drill before? Anyway, if I didn't or did I'm telling you now!

Every Tuesday at 4pm we have to don our Mae Wests – or life jackets as they call them – and take up positions on the deck. Those of us who are none too thin on top find ourselves crashing into people who appear yards away, talk about "maternal bosoms".

Another thing – this ship has a pair of albatrosses. (I'm sure that's spelt wrongly.) They have been with us ever since the Pitcairn Islands and at most times during the day we can see them wheeling round the ship in sweeping, graceful flight. Beautiful birds they are, and huge!

Well, now, I really have finished, so once more adieu, D.G.

[Continued on Monday 17 May 1954]

Well, I know I was supposed to have finished this, but I couldn't resist adding more to the letter.

As I mentioned before, we had our farewell dinner, and very nice too, all done proper like with a menu each, etc and etc. We have all been collecting autographs on the cards – menus I mean – and I have the Captain's and Chief Officer as well as all my friends and acquaintances.

Sketch of the Mae West life jackets.

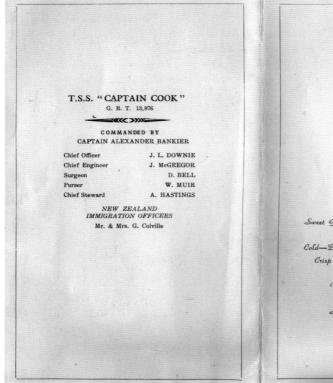

T.S.S. "CAPTAIN COOK"
G. R. T. 13,876

COMMANDED BY
CAPTAIN ALEXANDER BANKIER

Chief Officer	J. L. DOWNIE
Chief Engineer	J. McGREGOR
Surgeon	D. BELL
Purser	W. MUIR
Chief Steward	A. HASTINGS

NEW ZEALAND
IMMIGRATION OFFICERS
Mr. & Mrs. G. Colville

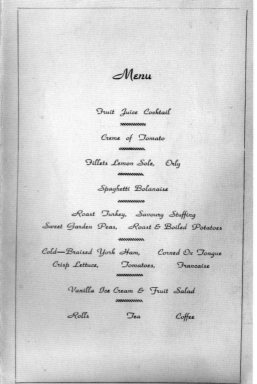

Menu

Fruit Juice Cocktail

Creme of Tomato

Fillets Lemon Sole, Orly

Spaghetti Bolanaise

Roast Turkey, Savoury Stuffing
Sweet Garden Peas, Roast & Boiled Potatoes

Cold—Braised York Ham, Corned Ox Tongue
Crisp Lettuce, Tomatoes, Francaise

Vanilla Ice Cream & Fruit Salad

Rolls Tea Coffee

Centre section of menu of farewell dinner. TSS *Captain Cook*.

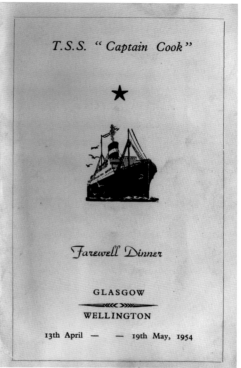

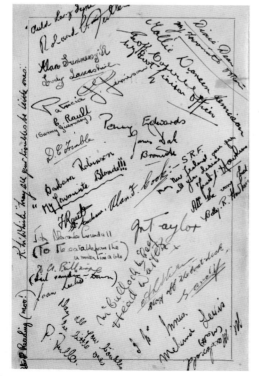

Above: Front and back pages of Dixie Dean's menu. The autograph half way down on the left is in Dorothy's handwriting: "Dorothy G Horne (My Favourite woman!)".

Left: Back pages of Dorothy Horne's menu. The autograph top right is in Dixie's handwriting "Dixie Dean (My Favourite Officer!)".

[The original Dixie Dean was William Ralph Dean, a famous English soccer player at the time. Since his nickname was Dixie, it became a common nickname for men with the surname of Dean.]

Furthermore, I have a date for June of next year. You see, I have been attending Farmers' meetings – there are so many farmers on the boat and they have fixed a date for a re-union next year. The chaplain is the Secretary and he's collected our names and will forward further details. Also I have several invitations to visit people when I am in their various areas. Isn't that nice!

We are really feeling like the "end" now. This morning we had a broadcast from the Wellington broadcasting station, just music you know, but still, it gives one a sort of feeling of being there! Actually we do arrive tomorrow, Wednesday the 19th remember, but I won't be leaving the ship until Thursday. Then I will know my fate. Somehow, one can almost imagine oneself sighting land – in actual fact we are travelling down the coast right now but we can't see it!

I can't tell you how I'm looking forward to receiving my mail – at least I PRESUME there will be some mail, I hope!

I have made up several little verses about the various members of our "gang"– I will maybe copy them out for you, though you won't appreciate them not knowing the people – however I will describe each one as I write out the poem.

Three of the five poems.

Dorothy has written on the back: "Dixie Dean, Alan Cook. 'Wide' John Taylor".

(1) Big John

Actually he is only as big as age is concerned – his age is eighteen but to hear him talk you'd think him 38 years. He is going out farming:

> *"Until he speaks, you'd think him shy.*
> *He's rather sweet, I can't think why.*
> *He talks so much.*
> *Someday a girl will take his eye.*
> *He won't talk then, I think he'll sigh.*
> *Don't you?"*

(2) Wide John

So called because he's so broad – he plays rugby, and talks like it. He also has a very loud voice and talks a lot. Furthermore he has a notorious appetite. He one day persuaded me to darn a pair of socks for him:

> *"Buy a pair of socks, dear John,*
> *That will not hole.*
> *Or find yourself a wife, dear John,*
> *Who'll sell her soul.*
> *'Tis said you like you food, dear John,*
> *That surely is not true!*
> *Cut out that second helping John,*
> *Your waist's enough for two."*

(3) Alan Cook

Well you know about him:

> *"A tower of strength, our Alan Cook.*
> *Think not to bend him with a look.*
> *He loves his work A1 and sheep.*
> *I do not think he would lose sleep.*
> *On mundane things!"*

(4) Dixie Dean

One of my favourites, I'm not sure whether I like him as much or more than Alan! No comment! He is a much travelled person born in Singapore and been all over the East. He likes playing solo whist, and is able to sit cross-legged on the floor like a yogi! He is a refrigeration engineer and a tool maker!

> *"Do you always play "solo" Dixie Dean?*
> *And sit cross-legged on the ground?*
> *Do you meditate on things unseen?*
> *Of parties and drink and places you've been?*
> *And your life's merry-go-round!"*

Photo of Dixie from Dorothy's photo album. Dorothy has written on the back: "Jordan 1952. (Just to see what he looked like – young and carefree!)".

Dorothy has written on the back: "This was taken in Wellington Harbour – on the *Captain Cook*." The photo was taken 19 April 1954. Dorothy is on the left. The other woman in the photo is Ann Hayman. The Haymans remained life-long friends.

(5) Alan from Blackpool

Nothing much to say about him. He's going into forestry.

> *"Oh where's the laddie from Lancashire?*
> *He's off to the woods I'm afraid my dear.*
> *To work with trees. That's why he's here.*
> *This son is done with fun I fear."*

There – that's how I amuse myself – with trivialities!
I have taken seven spools of film on this trip, some of them should be quite good.
I'm longing to see how they'll turn out! Roll on New Zealand!
I think I have come to the end at last. I can't think of anything more to say anyway for the moment, so this time it really is adieu.
As before,
Your Loving Favourite Relative!
Dorothy G.

The newspaper photo caption reads: "Four English nurses, who arrived in the city today to begin duties at Burwood Hospital, have their first meal in Christchurch – breakfast at the railway station. Left to right are: Misses Dorothy Horne (Yorkshire), Constance Hill (Manchester), Janet Snyer, and Beryl Holland, both from London." Courtesy Christchurch Star. 21 May 1954

[Letter dated 4 June 1954 written from the Nurses Home, Burwood Hospital, Christchurch, New Zealand.]

My Darling Mum and Dad and Family,

This is going to be one of the long letters, also I will be including some air mails I had left over, you can use them to write back to me!

I haven't received any letters from you lot as yet, but I mustn't get impatient – I expect there'll be some on the way. I have started correspondences with various people from the *Captain Cook* so I have had a few letters from various parts of NZ. That's managed to keep my head above water till I hear from you! Anyway, as I promised to write once a week, I thought I'd keep up the stream even though it's out of turn.

I hope also, you won't mind if I make this a joint letter to you all – and will you pass it round, Mum and Dad. Actually it's rather an expensive business to send long air mails so I'm going to make most of my letters to the family combined efforts. Mind you I will continue to write separately to Roy and Inez and Alan and Beryl, so my dear brothers and sisters, please don't get alarmed.

So far, I haven't anything exciting or new, to report – except that last Sunday I saw a sight I've never seen before. It happened that Dixie and I walked up a mountain

Dorothy has written on the back: "Looking down on Lyttelton Harbour – on the way up the Bridle Path."

path called the "Pilgrims Way" or the "Bridle Path" from Lyttelton harbour. It is the path taken by the Canterbury Pilgrims (the founders of Christchurch!) and leads up the Port Hills. They are very high up – and when we got to the top we could see right across the plain. The mountains formed the boundary in the distance and we could see the whole of Christchurch and the harbour and everything. On the other side we could see Lyttelton Harbour surrounded again by more mountains. Honestly – we were overcome. It was just like looking down from an aeroplane – I was thrilled to bits I can tell you.

Dorothy has written on the back: "Looking down on Lyttelton from Bridle Path 1954."

Mum and Dad, will you please include a cutting or two from the *Barnsley Chronicle* from that weekly article written in broad Yorkshire. You know the one I mean. My accent arouses great interest, so I'm cultivating it – and I promised to show one or two people how real broad Yorkshire looks written down. I wasn't able to visit that couple I mentioned in my last letter, because my off duty was changed to afternoon shifts. Anyway I'm going next week.

I intend to write a letter to the *Barnsley Chronicle* telling them something about this area, so don't be surprised if you see it in the paper – if they print it, that is!

There's one thing about this off-duty, it gives plenty of time for writing letters. I don't think there'll be any difficulty keeping up my correspondence.

I will enclose one or two snaps in this

Dorothy at Lyttelton.

letter, I haven't had any taken off the negatives yet so it will only be one or two – enough to be getting on with anyway, and so's you won't think I've forgotten!

I received my wireless and everything safe and sound – but it's not working just yet as I need a new plug – they have different plugs here. It works though, so don't worry! That's a bit of luck anyway – one or two of my girls have been unfortunate with their luggage and things being broken up in transit.

I was a trifle homesick the last two or three days – especially not hearing from anyone, but the odd letters from the various people I met on the way here helped to pacify me! Poor old Dorothy!

The weather is becoming more and more wintery – I can't get used to this weather business, everything seems topsy turvy. I keep thinking it ought to be Christmas soon. Goodness knows what it will feel like when it is Christmas!

I am buying Alan and Beryl's wedding present this week because I believe it takes ages for parcels to get home so I'd better get it off sharpish. Anyway I'll write as soon as I have posted it and you'll know it is on the way!

I can't put anything in the Post Office this fortnight because they hold back a week's pay for arrears and as I have the present to buy I just can't manage it. Anyway, I will be banking some of the next fortnight's pay so don't be alarmed. Incidentally, I have joined the superannuation scheme too – it isn't compulsory out here but it seemed like a good way to save, so I am doing it. By the way, what

OWD SAM SEZ

BEING THE WEEKLY MUSINGS OF A VETERAN TYKE WHO THINKS HE'S GOT IT ALL WEIGHED UP

T'other neet in't local, wi wor all 'avin a natter abaht Police Cooart fines. It wor generally agreed wi t' coompany present, as biggest sufferer theease days wor t' drivers. If t' fines wor owt t' judge wi, it wor reckoned as drivers mun bi classed as 'abitual criminals wi 'igh priority. Ah dooant knaw whether its reight, but Ahve bin telled afore, as the's that theer mony rules an reg'lations fo' t' rooad user, as t' minute feller drives aht on 'is ginnel, on'ta t' main rooad, 'ee commits an offence. Ahve offens wunnered misen, abaht theease 'ere magistrate chaps. Once thev med theear minds up who's telled likeliest tale, 'ow do the knaw 'ow much t' fine t'other feller. When a chap is med a J.P. an 'ee's new t' job does t' Clerk on't Coourt gie' 'im a list summat like a Buyers Guide at an auction, as lists all t' offences, together wi suggested penalties. Tha knaws, summat like this: Drunk an Disorderly, an Assaultin' a Bobby: Fust offence, Caution; Second offence, Gie 'im a rollicking; Third offence, One Pahnd; Failin' t' sign Drivin' Licence, One Pahnd; Side leet aht, Two Pahnd; Parkin' on't wrong side on't rooad, 'Ang up wi t' thumbs.

Whether its reight or wrong, wi finished up wi decidin', that if tha feels like kickin' ower t' traces, as far as t' law's concerned, tha waants t' leeave thi car in't garage, get thisen drunk, start a feight, punch a Bobby thru' a plate glass winder, an tha'll not onny 'ave a lot moar fun but appens tha'll bi i' pocket.

All this reminds mi on't two magistrate chaps who wor bahn whooam one neet fra a party. T' car brok dahn an the wornt another t' bi 'ad, soa, the borrer'd a tandem. When the wor ommost whooam, a Bobby stopped 'em fo' 'avin noa leet on't front. "Aham sewer yo'll ovverlewk it this time Officer," see t' chap as wor on't front, "Were Barnsla' Magistrates."

T' Bobby took is nooatbook aht, an said, "Sorry Sir, Ah 'ave t' do mi duty, Ah mun repooart yo'." (That last bit's a fairy tale, but it saands alreight). Onnyrooad, t' mornin' t' case cummed up, there wor nobbut t' same two magistrates on't Bench, an nubbdy else theer as could tak t' case. "What do wi do nah?" ses t' fust magistrate. "Tell thi what," ses t' second, "Thee try me an Ah'll try thee." "Reight," ses t' fust magistrate, an 'ee went dahn inta box. T'case wor read an t' magistrate in't dock pleeaded guilty. "Five bob," see t' magistrate on't Bench. Then 'ee got dahn an' the swopped places. T' case wor read ageean, an t' magistrate in't dock pleeaded guilty. "Ten bob," ses t' magistrate. "Aye up" ses t' other, "Ah nobbut fined thee five bob, an tha's fined me twice as much." "Ah thats reet," replied t' magistrate on' Bench, "But this is t' second offence of ridin' wiaht leets, Ahve 'eeard this mornin'."

Courtesy Barnsley Chronicle, 1954

One of the weekly articles in the *Barnsley Chronicle*, written in broad Yorkshire that Dorothy asked her parents to send so she could show her NZ friends how broad Yorkshire is written.

is happening about my insurance? Please let me know because it is important from the income tax point of view! I can send the money you know – we are allowed to send postal orders and I wouldn't forget! Whichever way is best suits me!

Well my very dear family – this is the end of my letter, don't delay with your replies will you. I live on letters!

Your Ever Loving Daughter

and Sister,

Dorothy G

P.S. Gosh wish I could bung you all in a plane – or better still on a ship 'cos you'd like that – and bring you all out here. That would be simply the loveliest thing.

[Letter dated 26 June 1954 written from the Nurses Home, Burwood Hospital, Christchurch, New Zealand.]

My Dearest Mum and Dad

I just received Mum's letter this morning and Dad's last week. I hope you do keep up the flow. You can't imagine what it means to have a letter from home!

From here in the sitting room I can see the mountains of the Southern Alps and it's impossible to describe how lovely they look. There is snow on the tops of most ridges now and they look just like something from a film. I wish you could see them.

The winter here is really just the job! These people don't know what a winter is like! Good old Whitsuntide – I hope Whit Monday was a better day than Sunday anyway! They don't have Whitsuntide celebrations here, instead what is Whit Monday to us is the Queen's Birthday here and people have the long weekend off just the same!

I have bought a woollen lamb for Chris and must get it off sometime. I still haven't bought Alan and Beryl's present as yet but I won't forget. I think I will have to send off a series of parcels soon marked for each person's birthday, Christmas etc. Apparently parcel post can be unreliable and take a long time! The trouble is you know what I am like with packing. What I will want here more than anything else is nylon undies, & etc – so if you should send me some, some time, Beryl knows what size I take in Kayses Bondon whatsitsnames!

If you do send me anything please put on the parcel "Gift – No Commercial Value" – make sure you label the things like that or I'll be squeezed by the Customs and I'd hate that. Just warning you! Someone in the Post Office will be able to give you details – whatever you do don't declare the real values of anything – always under £1! I'm telling you what the girls told me!

Last week I was as miserable as sin because I hadn't heard from anyone at home, but now that I have I'm feeling much better.

Inez has been hearing some unfortunate things about the cost of living out here and about how dead Christchurch is after 6pm. Well that's true but then you must all realise that wages are much higher than at home and the standard of living is better despite the cost of things! As for lack of entertainment – well that's very true but most people entertain at home and it's just a question of getting to know people – it takes six months usually to really settle in. Most of the settlers who came over with me are pretty miserable. I hear from some of them myself and some of the other kids hear from others so we keep contact with quite a lot of the "gang". Still we were told that we probably would be, so shouldn't take it too much to heart! Anyway I feel pretty cheerful just now so I'm not grumbling. As for booking for the pictures, frankly I think it's a good idea – much better than queuing. To me the scenery and the fresh air etcetera make up for a lot. Tonight I am going with Dixie to see "Midsummer Night's Dream" by the N.Z. Players.

I have heard from Inez too, she sounded a bit preoccupied in her letter – Gee I hate to think of Chris growing up and me not seeing her. I do hope you will all send me snaps now and then to remind me about her growing up – and of course ones of yourself!

I am enclosing one or two more snaps – for you – by the way I will be sending all the photographs to you Mum and Dad – I want you to give one or two out to Roy, Inez, Alan and Beryl – will you please – just as you like. I can't afford to send everyone reproductions so I will send you what I can afford! I am also enclosing some snaps of Mr and Mrs Frankland. They are a lovely homely couple, both Dixie and I have visited them and they made us feel really at home!

Next week will be the shortest day – funny isn't it – I know I keep harping on this summer and winter business but I just can't get used to it.

I am buying a bike for £15 from one of the girls who is going to Australia next month. As it is so flat around here and there is seldom a wind or breeze, cycling is in ideal pastime!

I can't see the mountains now, there's a bank of cloud over them! Later when the weather improves I'll try and take a photograph of them! It's a bit dull at the moment!

I'll write to Aunty Dolly and Uncle Ted when I finish this one to you – so set your mind at rest. You know I correspond with a lot of people – but I don't mind – as long as I receive regular letters I'll write until I am blue in the face!

Well Mum and Dad must close now – please don't forget – at least one letter a week. It doesn't matter what you write – even if it's what you had for dinner – it's all memories of home for me!

Your Loving Daughter

Dorothy G

[Letter dated 16 July 1954 written from the Nurses Home, Burwood Hospital, Christchurch, New Zealand.]

My Dear Mum and Dad

Time for a long letter again – and I have some more snaps to enclose! They may be repeats of previous ones I have sent, anyway you can give them to the rest of the family if they are.

Did I tell you about our tram cars here carrying persons on the front and back? They do look funny; one of these days I'll take a snap of them to give you some idea!

Incidentally your letter took 12 days to get here – they seem to take longer at this end for some reason, something to do with the air services I believe. Sometimes they catch the direct plane to NZ and sometimes they come through Australia.

I haven't heard from Vash – yet, I wonder why? My wireless is working okay thanks, but I can't seem to pick up many programmes on it, I suppose it's something to do with the dial. One of these days I'll have it adjusted! Alan tells me the weather is really bad still, I think I will have to transfer some of our sunshine to you – we could spare some I think. Mind you, it is cold, but the sunshine makes it bearable!

Talking about football (of course you know that to the New Zealanders "football" means Rugby Union), I mean soccer – we had an inter-island match last Saturday and as a South Islander I am pleased to be able to say that the South won 6-5. Soccer result figures tend to be astronomical in comparison with Home – but I believe the game is becoming more popular as more "new settlers" (that's us!) come out. Also, both rugby and soccer are amateur – they don't have professional teams out here.

Last Tuesday one of the girl's boyfriends took us on a drive around the bays around here and we thoroughly enjoyed ourselves. It is particularly interesting to see where the river enters the sea – forces a broad band of pale green water. As a matter of fact, when we were on the *Captain Cook* coming up the coast of South America towards the Panama, we could see from the colour of the sea where the rivers entered the sea!

By the way Mum – do you think you could acquire for me "Good Taste". You know, the magazine, for March, April and May – there is a series of articles in it I particularly want. Send them by ordinary post if you like – as long as I get them some time.

I think that's all for today – let's hope this letter doesn't take 12 days to reach you anyway. We are having another test in a fortnight – they certainly mean to keep us busy. I go into the operating theatre the week after next – I don't think it will be too bad – then one month on night duty – but then again, it's only eight hours a night, I don't mind all that much.

For the moment – cheerio,

Your Ever Loving

Dorothy G.

Dorothy has written on the back: "A view of the Nurses Home – I live upstairs."

[Letter dated 28 July 1954 written from the Nurses Home, Burwood Hospital, Christchurch, New Zealand.]

My Dear Mum and Dad

Another long letter! Also a few more snaps – repeats of some I've already sent, I think, but you can dish them around. Well Mum will be at home now and taking it easy I hope. Aren't you pleased Alan is a boy and therefore you don't have to worry too much about the wedding? See what a lot of trouble I'm saving you by remaining single!

You realise that I don't know the exact date of the wedding, I suppose, anyway Beryl and Alan will tell me. Beryl has given me details of the dresses and things! Should be quite a do! I hope you'll be well enough to enjoy yourself by that time. What a shame that it spoilt your holiday though – have you decided what you are going to do for your hols instead? Or are you still going to the caravan?

The bike is now mine and mine alone and I'm very proud of it. It's going to come in very useful anyway! I thought the photos Inez sent me of Christine were smashing, but where on earth has her hair gone to? It's about time she started sprouting by now! That little madam.

Nothing very exciting is happening these days, everything seems to have gone dreary, but life is like that isn't it? I expect next time I write everything will have brightened up or something!

Dorothy has written on the back: "Burwood 'crowd' outside Nurses Home. June 1954."

[Continued 29 July 1954]

Well things are brighter after all today – the weather is better to start with and I can see the mountains. There are a few of us in the sitting room discussing world affairs just like a UNO [United Nations Organisation] meeting!

I have changed my room and moved into the new Nurses Home amongst my friends. A much nicer room too, more room to put things and a bedside light so I don't have to pop out of bed to put it out now.

Yesterday I went into town with one of the girls meaning to do some shopping, but we just happened to pop into a bookshop. Well I'm afraid I didn't do any shopping. Instead I bought a cookery book of all things, a collection of English recipes from 1332 to 1932 with recipes from all the counties of England. It even tells you how to make haggis and how to jug a hare and things like that! Fascinating and of course utterly useless at the moment! Never mind, when I get my own flat some day I'll have a lovely time! This is one cookery book you won't have presented to you!

The other day I bought a tablet of Yardley's lavender soap and I nearly had a fit. It cost 5/-! If I'd known I'd never have bought it. I'm going to start cutting down on such luxuries – at 5/- a time anyway! I suppose it's because it is exported from England Home and Beauty!

Dorothy has written on the back: "Our dear old Home Sister. Burwood Hospital. May 1955."

You'll never guess the "newest" song out here – none other than "The Happy Wanderers". What's the latest at home? I don't suppose I'd know it if you'd told me, though, not for six months anyway!

There is a radiator outside my room and of course we always use it to dry things on. Well once a week Matron does a round of the corridors and half an hour before she's due the Home Sister does a round removing everyone's things. You can imagine the confusion! I found a pile of undies in my room the other day, none of them being mine. I'm going to keep my door locked on those days!

Incidentally Mum, Mr Butler told me you were an excellent patient and I'm very proud of you. In fact he said you were so good that you were 'masking' your own symptoms. There; now isn't that good? You will also have had your first inside glimpse of work in a busy hospital if Foundation Ward has been busy while you were there. I suppose it was, it usually is! Whitham's busier!

Well dear Mum & Dad, must finish now

Cheerio,

Love

Dorothy G.

[Letter dated 4 August 1954]

My Dearest Mum and Dad,

Your letter sent on 28th July arrived today so that means it took only seven days this time. Seems to be improving since Christchurch became an international airport – by international they mean that a plane flies in from Australia. Still, as even Australia is 1000 or so miles away, I suppose it qualifies! In this country people fly from one city to another – for instance from Auckland, Wellington, Hastings etc there are daily services by plane, and at quite reasonable prices too. People here are more air-minded I think from a civilian point of view, although of course they haven't the jets and things like at Home! England is Home here, always, and whenever that phrase is used people always know what you mean! Even to people who have never been to England and probably never will, it's Home!

Gosh, I'm glad you're at home, Mum; you had me worried I must say; now we will be able to compare scars! When I have written this letter I am going to write one to Alan and one to Beryl as the last ones they will receive separately, then after that it's Mr and Mrs! Exciting isn't it? I will be thinking about you all on Saturday 14th and will endeavour to put up a prayer for the happiness of my brother and new sister. No comments please!

The photos are lovely. I had bored everyone stiff by insisting they look at them and went into raptures about the one of my wee niece! She really is gorgeous. Too right! (That's an expression everyone round here uses – and so now I go around saying it – Too right!) Don't think I'll be back sporting a New Zealand accent though. If Mr and Mrs Frankland still talk broad Yorkshire after 34 years there's not much hope for me, is there?

Last weekend I met a lot of people in various homes and enjoyed myself thoroughly. It all came about through Dixie (he, him, his – male, you remember?!) meeting a widow at a club he belongs to and she invited him to her home, telling him to bring me along. Well we went there on Saturday afternoon and she took us in her car to some friends, then we returned to her house and stayed the night!

Dorothy and Dixie on a day outing to Cheviot, 70 miles north of Christchurch.

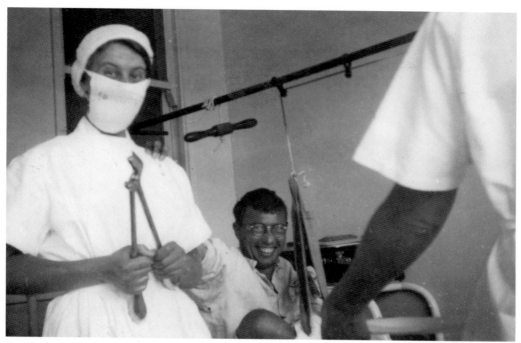

Dorothy has written on the back: "Fooling with 'Mac' (McFarlane – in with frostbite – rescued by Hillary on Himalayan expedition 1954). Burwood Hospital, N.Z. 1954."

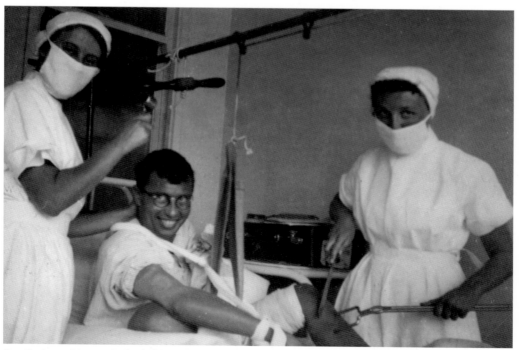

Dorothy has written on the back: "One of the Sisters & myself (I have to tell you in case you don't recognise me!) & Mac. Burwood Hospital, N.Z. 1954."

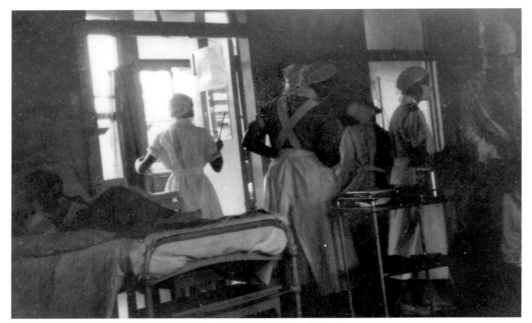

Ward 3, Burwood Hospital. 1954.

Then next day we went for a drive round some of the beauty spots and in the afternoon went and visited some more friends of hers. Dixie and I thoroughly enjoyed ourselves – and I was brought back to the hospital in the car! Mrs Marchard (we call her Isobel so I'll refer to her as such in future!) has a big house and gets rather lonely I think. Anyway she showered us with hospitality. There was one rather uncomfortable episode – at the first home we visited the host said to Dixie. "You sit there and your wife can sit beside you!" How we got around it I don't know because I was too busy cooling my blushing head under the cold tap (figuratively speaking!). I wondered if that would frighten Dixie off – and make him call it a day, but he has taken it in good part, and not mentioned it since! I don't think you need worry yourselves and your heads there – Dixie Dean is too much of a wanderer to think of settling down. I think he likes having someone to go out with, without emotional entanglements.

Sunday was the first day of spring and it's certainly true that some very exotic and odd looking NZ flowers are coming into bloom! Personally I can't wait to see a bit of green again. Winter bleakness of outlook seems to have been going on for years – but then I have had a year of it haven't I?

You will have received, and posted on I hope, the letter for Grandma. I didn't know where she would be when I wrote it, so I thought maybe you'd send it on! Also I knew that you would be pleased to see that I have written to her, it's a sort of joint family letter really for her to pass around, but really for her if you know what I mean. You can tell all aunts and uncles that I am being a very good girl indeed in answering all correspondence promptly, so if any of them would like to

Plastic Surgery Unit Class – Nov 1954. Dorothy is in the middle of the back row.

drop me a line I shall certainly answer at once – and would love to hear from them as you will guess!

Don't worry Mum and Dad, I fear your only daughter will finish up as a loving aunt – (spinster!). I don't think I will ever get married! I don't seem to have the right sort of temperament for settling down! Anyway Roy and Alan have done their duty in carrying on the family name – well, I must be careful there – I should say that I suppose Alan will do his duty someday.

As you will now know, I am in the Operating Theatre, and to tell you the truth, enjoying it! It's not half as bad as I feared and the staff working in there at present are very nice! Life isn't too bad really!

Talking about Vash – I am very surprised if he is getting married, but I should

Dorothy and Dixie's wedding. Dixie is wearing the Parachute Regiment "Wings" on his blazer.

Cutting the cake.

be hearing from him again soon so we will see. I am going to make no further comment on the matter at that moment. I still think a lot about him, but as you know, I'm not one for crying over spilt milk – and I'm here, and he's there, so it's no use being foolish about things is it?

There, now – you've had a really long letter in reply to yours – and I must now write to my brothers and sisters so cheerio my dearest parents, Mater and Pater.

Your Loving Daughter,

Dorothy G

P.S.

You will be receiving papers etc from Mr and Mrs Frankland. I hope you don't delay in writing to them. We haven't deserted them, by the way. Dixie and I are visiting them tomorrow. It's been a couple of weeks since I last saw them so it will be good to visit them again!

Incidentally just to refresh your memories, Dixie was on the *Captain Cook*, he comes from Devon, is a tool maker and fitter – was a parachutist (Red Beret) during and after the war and is about 27 or 28. I don't know exactly his age, I know it is about that! Okay? He was at one time to get married but his fiancée, a Swiss girl, was killed in a motor accident. The last bit I found out from Alan Cook (do you remember him?) by accident – he never talks about himself but carries her picture around in his wallet! Any more you want to know?

I find that I have two prints of each of two snaps so you can pass them on – even if you haven't had these particular ones, you have quite a lot of others. I just realised that I can't enclose them in an air mail, and I can't afford three 1/6 letters – as I am saving hard. I have put £5 in the P.O. this fortnight – so have to take it easy with forking out cash! Aren't I a good girl? I intend to put in £4 or £5 at least, every fortnight! We are paid fortnightly you know! Also I bought a windcheater which I need very badly with my bike!

On 3 June 1955, just over a year after first mentioning him and ten months after writing that neither she nor Dixie was the marrying kind, Dorothy and Dixie were married in Christchurch. They remained married until Dorothy's death in late 2004, less than a year off their Golden Wedding Anniversary. About 18 months later Dixie also passed away.

An article appeared in the *Barnsley Chronicle* during June 1955.

WEATHER STOPS £1 A MINUTE 'HELLO' TO THE BRIDE

Courtesy Barnsley Chronicle

Headline for an article that appeared in the *Barnsley Chronicle*, June 1955.

The article continued: "Bad weather today thwarted the attempt of a Mexborough woman to radio telephone her congratulations to her 26-year-old daughter who was married in New Zealand. Mrs Margaret Horne of Church Street, Mexborough, originally booked the call for midnight and was going to congratulate her daughter, Dorothy, before she was married at Christchurch, to Mr Arthur William Dean, a former Devonshire man.

"She was told last night that because of weather conditions, the call could not be obtained at that time, and she was asked to try again at 7 o'clock this morning.

"However, the same conditions prevailed and Mrs Horne patiently waited during the morning while two further attempts were unsuccessful.

"'We cannot reach New Zealand,' she was told by the operator at the International Telephone Exchange in London.

"£1 a Minute: Mrs Horne was told by the operator that if the call could not be put through before noon today – 11pm at New Zealand who are 11 hours ahead of Greenwich mean time – it could not be made again today.

Dixie's parents (left) and Dorothy's parents (right). Photo taken in July 1955, most probably Brighton, England. Dorothy has written on the back: "The people we would have most liked to have been here."

"As the minutes ticked by before midday Mrs Horne told a reporter: 'It has been an awful disappointment. We were making this little sacrifice to speak to our daughter,' she said, adding that the call would have cost £3 and £1 for every minute of conversation.

"Mrs Horne was doubtful whether or not she would attempt to make another call tomorrow because she did not know what plans her daughter had made for the honeymoon. 'She may have left Christchurch,' she said.

"Their daughter Dorothy emigrated 14 months ago. She began her nursing training at Mansfield Hospital and worked at a hospital in Surrey and Barnsley Beckett Hospital before leaving for overseas."

Nurse's Watch labelled with the name "Dorothy G Dean".

After working out their two-year "£10 Pom" bonds, Dorothy and Dixie worked for a time in Queensland, Australia before returning to New Zealand in April 1957. They then went on to farm in the South Island High Country and raised a family of four children. Dorothy did, however, return to nursing in the mid 1970s.

In late 1963, Dixie's parents sailed to New Zealand on the MS *Willem Ruys* for a long visit to New Zealand thus meeting their daughter-in-law and the first two of their grandchildren. This was the only visit they had an opportunity to make as Dixie's father passed away a few years later. In the late 1960s, Dorothy's parents immigrated to New Zealand from England and moved into a cottage on the farm. They sailed on the SS *Southern Cross*. Their coming enabled Dorothy to return to nursing. Later, when families were grown, both Dorothy's brothers made separate trips to New Zealand as did various nieces and nephews.

Illustrations acknowledgement

Except where otherwise acknowledged, all photographs and other original material were sourced from Dorothy or Arthur (Dixie) Dean's photo albums and other documents kept by them.

Members of the British Paratroop Regiment. Dixie is on the far left.

British Paratroop Regiment

On 22nd June 1940, Churchill called for the formation of a corps of at least five thousand parachute troops, suitably organised and equipped. A parachute training school was established and in February 1941 the first experimental raid was carried out in Southern Italy. A year later a successful attack was carried out by a Company of the Second Parachute Battalion and from then on the operations of the Parachute Regiment, nicknamed "The Red Devils" due to the red berets they now wore, grew in strength and scope.

Information from Dixie's 1952 Parachute Regiment Diary.

Royal Electrical and Mechanical Engineers (REME)

Dixie was a REME, as well as a paratrooper. The REME Corps was formed on 1st October 1942. Field Marshal Montgomery described them as 'Keeping the Punch in the Army's Fist'. REME officers and soldiers are fully trained combat soldiers in addition to their technical skills.

The REME motto is 'Arte et Marte' – By Skill and by Fighting.

There were two REME badges in the period Dixie served.

The first badge was designed in 1942 and consisted of a laurel wreath with the King's crown on top and a set of callipers inside the wreath. On the wreath itself there were four shields with the letters R.E.M.E.

In 1947 the 'Horse and Lightning' badge was adopted. The symbols on the badge are a flash of lightning, a horse, a chain and a globe. On the top of the badge is the King's (later the Queen's), crown. Underneath the crown are the letters R.E.M.E. The horse on the badge symbolises power while the chain symbolises controlled power. The globe symbolises the universal application of engineering and the lightning flash symbolises electrical power.

REME Information supplied with kind courtesy of the REME MUSEUM of TECHNOLOGY, Isaac Newton Road, Arborfield, Berkshire RG2 9NJ, United Kingdom. www.rememuseum.org.uk

Dixie's 1952 Parachute Regiment Diary. It is bound in red leather and has the Parachute Regiment Wings on the front cover.

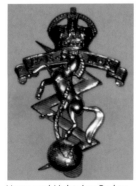

Horse and Lightning Badge.

CHAPTER 10

Fred and Pam Brown

Name	Frederick (Fred) and Pam Brown
Ship	TSS *Captain Cook*
Departure date	13 April 1954
Arrival date	19 May 1954 (disembarked 20 May 1954)
Destination	South Island
Marital status	Married

After war service in the Fleet Air Arm and having been in many countries, Fred Brown felt unsettled for some time, and this finally resulted in Fred and Pam leaving England in 1954.

Fred's war service not only made him unsettled, it also contributed to the choice of New Zealand as a country to move to. He had once been anchored near Picton, at the top of New Zealand's South Island. Following the end of the war in Tokyo Bay the ship was on

On the TSS *Captain Cook*. Pam and Fred are together on the right in the back row.

№ 18708

New Zealand Govt. Offices,
Migration Branch,
Carlton Hotel,
London, S.W.1.

THIS DOCUMENT IS NOT
VALID AFTER :

13 July 1954

NEW ZEALAND
DOCUMENT OF IDENTITY

Issued in lieu of a Passport for travel to New Zealand
as an approved migrant to :

Name ___Frederick Thomas Brown___

accompanied by his wife ___Pamela Brown___

DESCRIPTION :

	BEARER	WIFE
Nationality	British	British
Place of birth	Westgate on Sea, Kent.	Gillingham, Kent.
Date of birth	26. 5.23.	26. 9.28.
Height	5 ft. 10½ ins.	5 ft. 4 ins.
Colour of eyes	Blue	Hazel.
Colour of hair	Brown.	Brown.
Special peculiarities	None.	None.

CHILDREN

Name	Date of birth	Sex

SIGNATURE OF BEARER : *F.T. Brown.*

SIGNATURE OF WIFE : *Pamela Brown.*

M.C. Smith
Chief Migration Officer.

This document is valid for a single journey only and must be surrendered to the
Immigration Authorities at the Port of Disembarkation in New Zealand.

S.S. "CAPTAIN COOK"

BERTHING CARD

Name __Brown   Mr. F.T.__

Deck __B__

Section No. __—__

Cabin No. __116__   Berth No. __F.__

Please have this Card in your hand when you embark

FORWARD SALOON
SEATING CARD
1st SITTING

Table No.
½

Name *Mr & Mrs Brown*

ID document. Pam and Fred's New Zealand Document of Identity. At the bottom are their berthing card and seating card for the first sitting in the Forward Saloon.

Square dancing on the Prom Deck.

a goodwill tour to New Zealand. As a result of this visit, the Browns stayed in touch with a family from nearby Blenheim, and it was this family who nominated the Browns for the Assisted Immigration Scheme and who obtained a job for Fred.

These are Pam's memories of the voyage to New Zealand.

We were "£10 Poms", that is, "Assisted Immigrants", who paid £10 each and then had to work for two years on arrival or repay £86 each.

Fred and I were in separate cabins on the voyage out. Wives were separated from husbands, ladies together and men together. Teenage boys went with Dad, other children with Mum. However, we were both lucky in that we had good cabin mates.

We were six ladies in our cabin, counting me, Mrs Pam Brown. There was Mrs B, who was very fond of Canasta, and her daughter Yvonne. Her son was in another cabin with his Dad, Gordon. They were Welsh. There was a young girl, Margaret P, from Scotland who was quite lively. Whenever I see a tall man I can still hear her saying, "Och – he was tall – like a long drink of cold water poured into a suit". A mother and daughter Ann, also Scottish, made up our complement.

In Fred's cabin there were Mr H and his teenage son, Andy, from the Outer Hebrides I think (though they may have been from the Orkneys); Mr George H; and a rather loudmouthed man who worked for McAlpine refrigeration.

As all six in my cabin were on the first sitting for breakfast and other meals, we'd

Children's fancy-dress competition. Coincidentally, Janet Sealey, whose story is told in Chapter 12, can be seen on the far right (holding her numbered card).

spend five minutes each at the washbasin. Because water was rationed during the last three weeks of the trip when we were in the Pacific, the first person washed and dressed lined up for our rationed carafe of water.

Many of us would have liked to put about a dozen passengers over the side before reaching Wellington as they were arrogant and not good representatives of England. For example, they opted to sit in the aisles when for safety purposes they had been requested not to. One 'lady' wrote to the Panamanian Ambassador to complain that she had to use a knife instead of a jam spoon to get jam out of the dish!

I think the ship had been converted from carrying 500 to about 1160; so food supplies were awkward. Nevertheless, the food really wasn't bad. We had quite a nice older steward, a white Russian who would assume a Welsh, Irish, or French accent in order to obtain work in various places.

The weather was good although twice en route I had the sea sickness. If five of the six in the cabin were being sick, it was hard not to become the sixth! My husband's cabin had a pretty stewardess to attend them if necessary, but in our cabin we had a hard-faced old battleaxe.

We were issued with special soap which tried to lather in salt water.

Entertainment took the form of square dancing, a classical jazz session, PT, and a fancy-dress. However, since someone had been injured during the occasion on a previous trip, no crossing-the-line ceremony was conducted. We were given a

Fred with local
women.

Pam with local women and children with one of the ubiquitous large American cars parked behind them.

N.A.C. Heron Matapouri on arrival at Woodbourne, Blenheim.

coloured printed certificate for crossing the line, though.

On one occasion at a table behind us a group was drinking a toast to a birthday. When they opened the bottle of bubbly, it went off with a BANG. Fred leapt up and, holding the back of his neck, made out that the cork had hit him in the neck. Fred ended up with a free glass of bubbly to drown his sorrows.

At Curacao, Dutch East Indies, we stopped for oil – it was cheaper there – and the smell of oil permeated the air. We went ashore, and I particularly remember the homes, the vividly coloured flowers, and the very clean women and children. We were amazed to see huts with mud floors but with huge fridges and freezers, and cars that were almost new abandoned by the roadside for the most minor of problems.

The Curacao locals did not get on with the crew. Although it was a Sunday they had a fight with iron bars and other weapons – fortunately, it was after we returned to the ship. Some people ended up in hospital and one person died. It was quite a to-do. Apparently, fighting resumed each time the *Captain Cook* returned to Curacao. We were relieved to find that Panama City was much better policed and more upmarket.

At the dining table where Fred and I had our meals was a lass, Elizabeth P, a nurse from Essex, who had met us before travelling out so that she'd know a face or two. A friend who was to accompany her pulled out before the trip, and she nearly did, too, but her Dad said, "Haven't you any guts?" An aunt of hers knew my husband, so it was arranged that we would meet up in Canterbury in a cafe for a cup of tea. We travelled by train from Euston [in London] to Glasgow [Scotland where the shop sailed from] with her. After we disembarked at Wellington we never saw our friend Elizabeth again until 1983, when we paid a visit back to the UK. She had returned as a married woman with a family. Two of her sons have visited us, one who was born here in New Zealand, the other in the UK after Elizabeth's return home.

We disembarked in Wellington on 20 May 1954, and very shortly after were put on a bus to Rongotai airport [now Wellington airport]. The airport was in its very early stages with homes being shifted on lorries to make clear space for the airport. We were soon on a Devon aircraft bound for Woodbourne, Blenheim airport. A poster in a room at Blenheim airport was of Westgate Tower, Canterbury, UK, close to the street we just left.

My parents came to New Zealand on the SS *Southern Cross* in January 1957 and my brother came out on the *Captain Hobson* in June 1957. The *Captain Hobson* broke down five days offshore from New Zealand, an unnerving experience for most of the passengers. Luckily, my brother had been in the Boys Service in the Navy for ten years, and that helped him cope with the experience.

Over fifty years later, Pam and Fred still live in Blenheim. Pam left work after two years to have their first child, the first of three, but Fred stayed in his job with TH Barnes Ltd for 24 years.

Illustrations acknowledgement

All photographs and other original material was supplied by Fred and Pam Brown.

CHAPTER 11

Pauline Reynolds

Photo taken in 2006.

Name	Pauline Reynolds
Ship	TSS *Captain Cook*
Departure date	13 April 1954
Arrival date	19 May 1954 (disembarked 20 May 1954)
Destination	South Island
Age	13

Photo courtesy of Fred and Pam Brown

The TSS *Captain Cook* being helped away from the wharf at Glasgow. The left hand tug is the *Flying Eagle*. April 1954.

I was thirteen years old when we sailed from Glasgow on the TSS *Captain Cook* on 13 April 1954. We had travelled over to Glasgow from Belfast the night before on one of the White Star Line ferries. The morning had started out cool and wet, but the weather improved during the day so that by afternoon the skies had cleared. We sailed down the Clyde past famous shipyards like John Browns and out to sea in gorgeous sunshine.

Our route took us down to the Bay of Biscay and then west across the Atlantic to San Cristobal in the Dominican Republic, Curacao, and Colon, the entry to the Panama Canal.

The ship under Captain Brown was a converted troop carrier. She was more than 30 years old. She had a single funnel and two masts and accommodation for over 1000 passengers. Most of the crew were Scots, but there were some New Zealanders who were working their passage back home. Our first disappointment was the discovery that we were to be split up as a family – we had hoped to be able to travel together. Dad was allocated to a cabin with five other men whilst Mum and I joined four other women. Apparently people with young children were able to travel together, but the mix of single passengers and families didn't fit the available cabin space. I suppose also that the owners were trying to squeeze as many bodies on board as possible. Our cabins were in the same corridor and not too far apart, so that was a blessing.

Photo courtesy of Phyllis Young

On the Clyde departing from the Glasgow docks, looking from the stern of the ship. April 1954.

Photo courtesy of Carol Symington

The After Dining Saloon on the TSS *Captain Cook*.

Photo courtesy of Dorothy Dean

Large tarpaulins were rigged across the deck to provide shade for the passengers.

As we sat around on deck in the warm spring sun waiting for the crew to finish loading and depart the Glasgow docks, we couldn't help noticing a family on the wharf having great difficulty saying goodbye. Some relatives had come to farewell the family of four, but when it came time for all passengers to be aboard and all visitors to disembark, the wife refused to board. As a result, the family was left looking rather forlorn on the dock as we pulled away – with their luggage presumably still in the hold. I have often wondered what happened to them.

The ship's desalination equipment didn't work well. It meant that showers were inclined to be on the salty side. Mum was not amused.

For meals we sat at a table for 12 and by the time we were a few days into the voyage we had got to know the others reasonably well. Our stewards were a Scot from Glasgow and a young New Zealand man named Cliff who was working his passage back home. His home town was New Plymouth. He had been studying drama and acting in Britain.

We enjoyed the food, although it began to get a little boring after several weeks. The ship's cook was an expert bread-maker. He made wonderful scones and excellent bread rolls, fresh for every lunch and dinner. The farewell banquet held a day or so before our entry to Wellington featured turkey on the menu.

We celebrated Easter on board ship somewhere in the Atlantic Ocean. The Protestant chaplain was a Methodist. He was overshadowed by the Catholic chaplain, a young enthusiastic priest who arranged more activities, including

Lenten Services, than the Methodist man did and got an amazingly good turnout to these events.

At each stop bus tours were laid on for those who wished to see something of the local sights. The Caribbean ports we visited were interesting for the mix of ethnic groups and the number of older American cars in the streets. They seemed to be 20 feet long!

I recall our passage through the Panama Canal towed by the 'mules' in the canal itself and in other places sailing across a vast expanse of lakes. I remember the system of locks used to raise and lower the ship. I had been expecting that in the higher parts of the canal the surrounding forest would be lush and tropical but it wasn't: it consisted of scrubby shrubs, not particularly attractive. The atmosphere was very hot and oppressively humid. Large tarpaulins were rigged across the deck to provide shade for the passengers.

There were quite a number of options for entertainment during the voyage. In the evenings there were dances, concerts, quizzes, card evenings, talent quests and fancy-dress parties, and a number of slide evenings depicting the beauty of New Zealand. Musical appreciation classes were held. During the day, deck games were organised. The ship had a small library and I seem to recall that it was possible to borrow books from it. I think that we could also borrow board games. Monopoly was a great favourite – we played it for hours on end. Tours of the engine room

Photo courtesy of Dorothy Dean

One of the life boats. The cinema screen was erected on the poles in the background on the right.

Photo courtesy of Phyllis Young

Storm on the Pacific.

were laid on for those who enjoyed such things. Life boat drills were held every Tuesday afternoon and taken very seriously.

A few days after leaving Balboa, the exit to the Canal, there was a Crossing the Line ceremony in the Pacific Ocean. We were duly visited by King Neptune and his retinue. Some young people were selected for a dunking in a briny canvas pool set up on deck to the accompaniment of much hilarity. The ship didn't possess a proper swimming pool.

Some of the women clubbed together to organise school lessons in the mornings for the younger children. The children in one family I recall were kept at their lessons by their father who was a secondary school teacher and education college lecturer. A good many years later the oldest boy Clark and I found ourselves together at Dunedin Teacher's Training College. When I asked him if the lessons on the ship had been helpful, he replied that only the maths and English had been because he had had to take different subjects at Otago Boy's High.

There were some interesting characters on board. One was a young nurse who sported the longest cigarette holder I'd ever seen. We kids thought that she looked so-o-o elegant and sophisticated. She was headed for Waikato Hospital in Hamilton to work.

Jerry and Ralph were a couple of mates in their 20s who were seated at our table. Jerry was short and stocky, Ralph taller and thin. One morning at breakfast,

Photo courtesy of Arthur Dean

Wellington city and harbour.

Jerry asked: "Did you hear about the fight last night?" Apparently he had become aware of a disturbance in the next cabin quite late at night and on investigating had discovered a bout of fisticuffs in progress. It turned out that the occupants of the cabin had returned late in the evening to discover an intruder ransacking their belongings. The fight was their attempt to restrain the thief. Which they did, and he was duly hauled off by the ship's policeman to the brig – presumably for the remainder of the voyage.

We sailed past Pitcairn Island during daylight hours without stopping. We could see it quite clearly in the distance. The Pacific Ocean was a huge expanse. We looked out for flying fish, albatrosses and the occasional ship heading back towards Panama.

I seem to recall that we had a brief breakdown and drifted for a few hours while repairs were made, but I can't recall where that happened. We encountered heavy weather on a couple of occasions in the Pacific. During one of these storms I missed my footing on a companionway and twisted my ankle badly enough to visit the ship's doctor to have it strapped. The passengers all seemed to disappear at mealtimes during storms.

A boy baby was born during the voyage. I recall blue balloons decorating the doorway to the ship's hospital to celebrate his birth.

Landfall off New Zealand on a cold day revealed a coastline shrouded in mist and rain. We sailed down the East coast and into Wellington Harbour. The date was 19 May 1954. In those days it was a very busy harbour with lots of marine traffic.

The steepness of the surrounding hills on which the city was built fascinated us. The houses seemed to be sitting on top of each other. It was so picturesque from the harbour as the lights in the hill suburbs began to come on as evening fell. We were unable to berth that evening so anchored in the channel. Officials arrived on board and began the process of immigration and customs checks to smooth out our disembarkation.

Next morning we berthed at the overseas terminal. Nearby was a freighter loading meat from a train on the wharf. It was all done by manual labour: each frozen carcass being hefted by a water-sider up the gangplank onto the deck and from there into the holds, all in the open air. The wharfies were dressed in singlets and shorts. They must have been pretty fit to climb up the gangplanks all day with their loads of meat. Food handling regulations were clearly very different in those days to what we have now. The meat was most likely destined for the United Kingdom from whence we had come.

My cousin Betty Taylor, who was living in Palmerston North at that time, arrived a little later in the morning and took us on a tour of inner Wellington. To us it seemed a very compact city with narrow streets and a sense that everything was crowded together. Trams were still running: single-deckers, not the double-deckers we had been used to in Belfast.

At the end of the day we went back on board the ship for dinner and were then escorted by bus to the inter-island ferry wharf where we boarded the ferry *Maori*. We sailed for Lyttelton about 9 pm, arriving there about 7 am. We disembarked onto the boat train on the wharf that took us through the long tunnel to Christchurch station.

We had breakfast in the cafeteria at the station before joining the express to Ashburton. Here again was something new. The carriages on NZ trains had a central corridor and one could walk from one end of the train to the other through doors at the ends of the carriages. British carriages of the time had compartments. The landscape of the Canterbury Plains we entered after leaving Christchurch was flat and brown. We couldn't see the Southern Alps that day because of low cloud. I was amazed at the width of the Rakaia River, the number of channels and the deep aqua blue of the water in them. There was nothing like this in Britain. There seemed to be pine plantations everywhere ... and the sheep! We'd never seen anything like it.

It was raining when we arrived in Ashburton. We were met by local immigration officials and by our cousins who lived there and who were primarily responsible for Mum and Dad's decision to head for Ashburton in the first place. It had been more than two years since we had all seen each other so there was plenty to talk about! Our belongings were soon loaded into their cars (all older models, I noted) and off we went for a drive around town.

Ashburton was a huge contrast to Belfast. It had a population of about 8000 whereas Belfast had about 125,000 at that time. We noticed that there were bikes everywhere. I remember my mother asking plaintively after we had driven down the main street: "Is that all there is?" How everyone (except her) laughed! Mum clearly thought she had come to the back of beyond. She had a very difficult time adjusting to life in New Zealand and she never really thought of it as 'home'. However, with the passage of time she made a number of very close friends and these she loved dearly.

On the other hand, Dad settled into the New Zealand scene very quickly and never looked back. He found work as a textile engineer at the Lane Walker Rudkin Woollen Mill.

Mum made several trips back to the 'old country', but Dad never did. When he left Northern Ireland he had told his mother: "I'm never coming back." He never regretted his decision to emigrate to New Zealand.

For my part, I readily embraced and have thoroughly enjoyed the Kiwi lifestyle.

While I was a teacher trainee at Dunedin I met my husband, David Richmond, a medical student. We had two children and 42 years of happy married life.

Illustrations acknowledgement

Except where otherwise acknowledged, all photographs and other original material was supplied by the Richmond family.

BIG MIGRANT DRAFT FOR S.I. ARRIVES

The inter-island steamer Maori to-day brought 257 British immigrants and 30 airmen from Wellington.

The immigrants arrived at Wellington on Wednesday afternoon in the migrant ship Captain Cook, which left Glasgow on April 13 with 1180 passengers. These included 200 children and 60 wives who have come to New Zealand to join their husbands.

Of the total who arrived in Lyttelton, 151 left by the two southern expresses this morning. Some of them will stay in Rakaia, Ashburton, Timaru, Oamaru, and Dunedin. The party included a number of married couples with children.

Many Tradesmen

Twenty-seven of the draft will stay at the Tasman Hostel. Nine women were sent to the Hansons Lane Hostel. Those who are going to Dunedin will live in transit house units at Milton.

The new-comers include engineers, builders, carpenters, plasterers, painters, auto-machinery and radio mechanics, footwear workers, factory and farm hands and domestics. There are also four nurses for the Burwood Hospital.

Mr R. H. Bell, from the Labour Department, travelled with the immigrants from Wellington. They were met by other representatives of the Labour Department.

Courtesy Christchurch Star 21 May 1954

CHAPTER 12

Janet Sealey

Name	Janet Sealey
Ship	TSS *Captain Cook*
Departure date	13 April 1954
Arrival date	19 May 1954 (Disembarked 20 May 1954)
Age at departure	13
Destination	North Island

This chapter begins with extracts from letters written to the Sealey family (Janet and her parents, John and Grace) before they left England from Janet's Uncle George and Aunty Grace, and their friends Fred and Nell Anstey. Both these families had already moved to New Zealand in 1952 and 1953.

They give an idea of the sort of information the family had received about New Zealand before they embarked on their voyage to the other end of the world.

These are followed by extracts from a letter received by the family while they were on board the TSS *Captain Cook*, before Janet gives her recollections.

The two appendices at the back of the book contain material relevant to the Sealey family. The first appendix contains two letters from people the Sealey family would be leaving behind in England, written before the Sealey family sailed. The second appendix covers the process of applying for assisted immigrant status to the Sealey family's arrival in New Zealand.

Extracts from letters received by the Sealey family before leaving England

[Letter to Mrs G Sealey from Mrs E Anstey, Birkenhead, Auckland, New Zealand, dated 22 March 1953.]

Dear Grace and Hubby,

We are, as you know, very happy and contented out here in our new life. At first it was so strange not knowing anybody but I would hate to have to leave here now. The people are most kind and friendly. We have never earned money so easily before in our life, as hard work and worry is not known out here, believe me.

I know as soon as Grace and George get in their own house, which is going through by the way, they are going to nominate you three. It only took ten months

Photo taken the day the TSS *Captain Cook* docked in Wellington. Right to Left. Janet's father (John Henry Sealey), Janet, Janet's mother (Grace Margaret Sealey), Ada Morton who, with her step-daughter, shared a cabin with Janet and her mother and one other mother and daughter.

from the time we nominated my brother and his family until the time they sail, which is 1 May 1953. I don't think it will cost the four of them a penny for the fares so it will give them a good start. All I hope is that they can sell in time as New Zealand House only gave them ten weeks' notice.

When you do hear from New Zealand House your Hubby will be asked for three references, so as soon as George writes and tells you he has been for the forms for your nomination, try and get things ready over your side as it helps a lot.

I don't know if Grace told you what lovely weather we are having out here. It is never what you back home know as cold, and I for one am very pleased about it. Fred is very fit and happy at his job. He leaves the house at 7.10 each morning laughing from ear to ear. He takes this life all as a joke. My son Terry has grown into a very nice lad and next year we hope to see him at High School.

We have booked our passage to come back home for a visit. We hope to fly to Sydney on November 6 1953 then travel by sea to England. I think that it's a waste of good money as it is to cost £300 for us three each way, but Fred said we have worked hard for it so we should enjoy it. But it is daft as we only intend to stay back home for **six weeks**. I am trying hard to put Fred off the idea.

Fred, Terry & Nell.

[Letter to Mrs G Sealey from George Hodgkinson, Birkenhead, Auckland, New Zealand, dated 20 February 1954.]

Dear Grace and John,

I bet you are either getting excited or anxious now you have heard you have been accepted. They notified us you will be sailing about April – May. That means you will arrive here about June. It will be winter time so expect plenty of rain.

Now what are you doing about your home (furniture)? I know it is pretty expensive to bring things out here – my home cost about £200 – but if you have good things including say your piano, you won't replace them anything near the price you will sell them for in England. I think you will be allowed twenty cubic ft each – that is 60 cubic ft all together. Try and get tea chests for this free allowance, and you can pack china, linen and all manner of things in them. **Don't** start giving parts of your home away. I'm not telling you to be mean, but even a pudding basin has got to be bought out here, the same as in England.

If you can do it, bring interior spring mattresses. I bought four and brought them out for £20. Out here they cost over £20 each. Prices are high here, but if you are prepared to work there is plenty of work and good wages. But starting in a new country you want to save hard.

If John has a decent suit or so it's enough. You won't want a heavy overcoat but all of you want **good** raincoats. The winters are often wet and chilly but not really cold. As for the summer, a pair of shorts is enough in the weekends. Try if you can to bring some decent shoes, as good shoes are dear. Quality comes before show, as our roads are rough.

Don't be scared of Customs here, they are okay to immigrants. Let me warn you, like all newcomers you may be disappointed in many things, but after the first year you will think it a grand country.

So cheerio love & all.

George and family

[Included with the letter was a note written by Grace, George's wife, listing the items she would like purchased and brought out for her from England. It included 1 dozen pillow slips, 6 pairs of sheets , 6 towels, 1 pleated skirt, 1 black suit size 36, preferably with 2 skirts and a blouse to go with it, 1 pleated skirt. Suits were "very dear here, £20 and I can't afford that". She also asked them to bring a summer dress from Marks and Spencers for a friend.

Grace added: "Bring plenty for yourselves and John will need a nice Mac and stout shoes for our rainy season. Umbrellas are about £2, so if Marks are cheap get one for yourself."]

Letters received by the Sealey family during the voyage

[Letter to Mr and Mrs Sealey from George Hodgkinson, dated 16 April 1954.]

Dear Grace, John & Janet,

I hope this letter catches you up all right at Panama. I suppose by now you regard yourselves as old salts! If I had thought before I would have told you how to get around Panama City if you stopped there. We always remember it for the banana splits at the YMCA, where you could also buy dollars.

Well, now you will have a long sea run, about three weeks, across the Pacific and then New Zealand. It's a pity you are arriving in the winter but there will be no snow or fog.

I have been out fishing today on the harbour (Good Friday), and it was rather poor sport and plenty of rain. I suppose I would have looked strange to you, in oilskin coat and bare feet, walking through the streets. We had eight fish, enough for a feed. Last Saturday we had 35. They weighed a hundredweight and a half and nearly killed us coming up from the beach. I bet John will have to learn to fish. In any case he'll come in handy helping me to build a boat this winter.

Michael is spending the Easter on a friend's farm so we are pretty quiet as the weather is bad. Tomorrow we go to the local pictures. By the way you'll be seeing pictures you saw back home for the next 12 months, but the cinemas in town are quite modern and have had the Cinemascope for about six months.

I don't know if you have been informed that when you arrive at Wellington they do everything for you and you will soon be on the train for Auckland. It's a night express and takes about 14 hours – a cow of a ride so have a shilling pillow to rest on. I'll be at the station to meet you. So cheerio for now.

Love George and family

Janet's recollections

My parents and I emigrated to New Zealand leaving Glasgow on 13 April 1954 and arriving in Wellington on 19 May 1954. We were a very close family and I left behind my grandmother, aunts and uncles and numerous cousins. I knew a little about New Zealand from my uncle George who had already emigrated, and we also had some information from New Zealand House. Moving to New Zealand completely changed my life. I left behind all my school friends and cousins for a new life. Of the people we knew well on the boat, our cabin mates, none returned to the UK to live.

The trip took about five weeks. On the ship there was always something going on, such as sweepstakes, games, dances and films. A big screen was set up on the deck and we watched under the stars. There was a 'writing room' which was a nice quiet space. The ship's library had a lot of books about New Zealand and I think that there were talks about what to expect when we arrived in New Zealand.

I wasn't bored on the trip. Overall it was a very happy experience.

There were two stopovers on the trip from England to New Zealand. One was at Curacao and the other at Panama. At Curacao some of us went to a very large (I presume public) swimming pool and had a great time. When we arrived in Panama there was a parade of some kind in progress. The people were very friendly and seemed very attractive.

After docking at Wellington, New Zealand, we travelled by train to Auckland. I was surprised at the variety of food available. My parents were astonished that

Written on the back of the photo. "Janet as a flapper in the fancy-dress competition. The 'Carmen Miranda' next to Janet is a boy. Janet recalls – "I remember when in fancy-dress the Captain asked 'Who taught you to sashay like that' and I replied 'My mother'. She certainly encouraged me to do so on that occasion!" This is the same fancy-dress competition mentioned in Fred and Pam Brown's story in Chapter 10.

'Cabinmates.' From Left: Ada Morton, Win and Bill Johnson's daughter, Fred Morton, Win Johnson, Bill Johnson, Grace Sealey, John Sealey, Janet Sealey. Photo taken at Win and Bill Johnson's daughter's 21st, Mangere, Auckland, New Zealand. 1961

on the train they could buy beautiful corned beef sandwiches for only 4d each. On that trip we stopped at Frankton Junction and when we got off there was tea, cakes and buns supplied for us all.

I remember my first day at Northcote College. Everything seemed very casual. I was used to an all-girls Grammar School in England, which was quite different. By contrast, my mother and I thought it a great joke that when we went to town on a Friday evening all the ladies were wearing hats and gloves. This seemed very strange to us; it seemed that people were overdressed.

For a while after we arrived we had clothing items sent from England. Shoes in New Zealand were not of very good quality. However things did improve through the years.

My family stayed in touch with some of our shipmates for many years.

I met my future husband, a New Zealander, at a dance in Auckland City. I married at the age of 19 and had the first of three daughters when I was 21. I now have five grandsons and three granddaughters. As those cousins say who come from large families and only have one grandchild, "Not bad for an only child".

I missed my relatives and did occasionally have regrets about coming to New Zealand. Many years after arriving in New Zealand I returned to England for the one visit, to see my daughter and son-in-law while he was studying in the UK.

Illustrations acknowledgement

Except where otherwise acknowledged, all photographs and other original material were supplied by Janet Haines (nee Sealey).

CHAPTER 13

Anne Dover

Name	Anne Dover
Ship	MV *Ruahine*
Departure month	June 1954
Arrival date	8 July 1954
Destination	North Island
Marital status	Single
Profession	'Housemother' in children's homes
Intention	To remain in New Zealand

I don't really know why I left the UK. I'd served in the WRNS [Women's Royal Naval Service] during the war and, like many others, found it hard to settle down. We were a reasonably close family and I left behind my parents, married sister, and various aunts, uncles and cousins on both sides of the family.

I came out under the auspices of the Society for the Overseas Settlement of British Women. They made it easy and they got me a job in New Zealand. I don't recall much paperwork. I knew a little about New Zealand and once I got here I didn't think of leaving.

I came out on the MV *Ruahine*. We left from London in June 1954 and arrived in Wellington on a Sunday about six weeks later. There were about 250 passengers but the only other migrant passenger was a young man I didn't meet until we disembarked in Wellington. I shared a cabin with a girl in her late teens who was returning to New Zealand with her parents. We became friendly and went on shore leave together, but although they telephoned to check that I had arrived safely at the Children's Home (my destination), we didn't stay in touch for long after we arrived in New Zealand.

I enjoyed the trip, never got bored and retain some vivid memories of the voyage: going through the Panama Canal, the blue blue of the tropical ocean, flying fish, and the Pitcairn Islanders coming out in their longboats to sell souvenirs! (I believe the boat dropped off stores to the Pitcairn Islanders.)

When the other migrant and I arrived, we were met by a representative from the Department of Labour – it was a Sunday, and he wasn't very happy about working on that day! He told us what to expect on our forthcoming train journey north; about the 'bun rush' refreshment stop and hiring of pillows for one shilling. The other migrant and I walked the empty streets of Wellington until it was time to get to the train. We were met off the train in Auckland by another chap from the Department of Labour. He took the young man to the Mangere Migrant Hostel and then me to the children's home in Papatoetoe where I had a live-in job as a house mother.

It was not easy to have a social life in that kind of work, but I joined up with the Auckland branch of the ex-WRNS UK Association, and visited a couple in Pukekohe who had been billeted with friends of my parents – he'd been in the New Zealand Air Force, and my parent's friends had given me their address.

On the ship coming out I particularly remember **white** bread rolls and **white** bread. It was the same in New Zealand, as was the liberal use of butter.

I missed Marks and Spencers, though, for buying reasonably priced clothing of reasonable quality. I also found it difficult to buy earrings for pierced ears.

Although I had only been bonded for two years, I ended up staying at the children's home nearly four. After I left there in 1958 I took a job as a Matron at Huntly School (a boys' preparatory school) in Marton [where Anne still lives]. It was a pleasant change to have well-disciplined youngsters and I remained there for 14 years. I also took holiday jobs, mainly housekeeping on farms, and saw a lot of New Zealand in that way. I was surprised at first by the length of some of the drives to the farms and the use of mail boxes at the end of the drives. I was also surprised at people going barefoot inside their houses and children going barefoot to school.

Eventually I got tired of the institution life and got a job housekeeping for a widower farmer and his children just out of Marton. I was quite a good yard dog at times! I stayed with the family for about 30 years, and even though I have retired now I still have plenty of contact with the youngsters from the farm and their children.

I am very glad I came and settled in New Zealand.

CHAPTER 14

Catherine Hill

Name	Catherine (Cathie) Hill
Ship	TSS *Captain Cook*
Departure date	12 July 1954
Arrival date	15 August 1954
Destination	South Island
Marital status	Married
Profession	Secretarial/ office (after becoming a widow)
Intention	To remain in New Zealand

We left Scotland because the opportunities for work post-war were very limited. My husband had a sister in Dunedin, New Zealand, whose husband was able to get sponsorship for him through the company he worked with. Assisted immigrants had to have a surety of work. We were "£10 Poms" even though we were Scottish! As a married woman there was very little paperwork for me – my

Family farewells at the railway station near where Cathie's husband's family lived in Scotland. From left: Cathie's father-in-law, Cathie and little Catherine, her mother-in-law, her husband Alexander Hill. Polmont, Scotland, 1954.

The newspaper caption reads "Following Captain Cook in the *Captain Cook* on a trip to New Zealand is Mrs A. Hill from Bo'ness, and one year old Catherine. They have a last British snack before embarking. July 1954." First published in *The Bulletin*.

SAILING AWAY

daughter and I travelled on my husband's passport.

I left behind all my family – although I had an aunt-in-law in New Zealand, I didn't know her before coming to New Zealand. My husband left behind his two brothers, Mum and Dad, and one sister and her family. His sister later came out to New Zealand. All my family remained in Scotland – not one of them ever came out to New Zealand, even for a visit.

We were a reasonably close family although we all had our differences and went our own ways within Scotland. My daughter Catherine [now Cathy Stevens] remembers getting wonderful gifts; she particularly remembers a watch that came in a glass/plastic slipper and had a Cinderella on the face, and the traditional tube of Smarties. Her grandmother saved her coupons at the co-op where she spent her money for presents.

I didn't want to leave home and leave my aging and sick mother behind, but I had to follow my husband. At age 30 I was not a child, but it is never easy to leave all you know and come to an unknown. It was made even harder because we all expected the move to be permanent – in those days it was hard to imagine being able to afford to uproot again. My mother was a strong woman, and I believe she would have dug her toes in about my going if she couldn't handle our separation. I did not know much about New Zealand before I arrived. I had had some communication with my husband's sister and family so knew something about Dunedin, the city I was coming to. I also read a lot, and gleaned quite a bit that way.

For someone who had never been on a ship cruise, the trip out was a novelty! There were about 1045 passengers on board, and there seemed to be more women than men – maybe because of war brides from the UK coming out to New Zealand to be with their husbands who had been de-commissioned in New Zealand. Other

The Hill family on board
the TSS *Captain Cook* 1954.

Forces families came from Commonwealth countries such as India, and the many single men and women may have been hoping to come out to a better life.

There was plenty to do if you wanted to (or could) join in: swimming pools, deck games, bars to socialise in, or different card games – most of these activities were more suitable for singles or couples without families. It was a bit more difficult to socialise if you had children – even socialising over a meal at night was difficult. Your child ate first at a children's meal and then you had to leave them to go and have yours. You had to leave your cabin door open so that the stewards could keep an eye on the babies – the doors were so big and heavy that you were not supposed to leave children closed in behind them. You then had to take turns to go and check through your meal – that's the way we felt, anyway. We felt we couldn't leave our daughter on her own for a couple of hours each night without checking. Any staff on board who had to do penance duty were roped in to feed the children

– they did not like doing this job, as their attitudes showed! – and I must admit the noise and chaos could be pure hell. However, the crew got right in behind some of the other on-board activities. For example, they were judges at the dress-up events. I never got bored during the voyage – time passed as a routine kicked in.

As a small family we were fortunate to have a cabin that contained two bunks and a cot. We were also very lucky to have a cabin with easy access to the outer deck – we were on Deck One. Young couples without a family were split up – I suppose you could pack more people in if they were segregated four to a room at least – but it would have been very difficult for them. I remember one couple who came along to a dress-up night as two bunks. They entitled their outfit 'Frustration through immigration'!

The food was wonderful. It was all prepared and brought to you and the quality was excellent. We did not have to pay for our travel – everything was supplied. (We were assisted immigrants, after all.) The only people who complained were some of the colonial service families that had obviously experienced service and servants.

Travelling with a young child meant that washing was a regular daily routine. There were no disposable nappies in those days. You had to find your niche in the daily routine, as some of the ex-colonial women demanded and got services ahead of you. You had to get in the know, and if you greased the palms of a few staff you could get access to tea-making facilities and other small niceties and take them back to your room.

Little Catherine introducing herself to two young boys. The man is holding a box brownie camera, the same type of camera as these photos were taken with.

Crew members, in tropical whites, judging at a dress-up event. Quite a few nurses are amongst the judges.

We were able to leave the ship in Curacao; I think it was only for the day. We didn't go far on land as, having a small child, we had to get taxis, and it was also the rainy season. But everyone we met ashore was welcoming, and we were a curiosity with our little baby – she was the focus of attention.

As we approached New Zealand I had all the feelings you would expect from someone approaching another unknown, but it was a relief to disembark, even though we still had another leg of travel to face. We had to stay on board the first night in Wellington as we were to board the inter-island ferry for our trip over to the South Island the next day and then on down to Dunedin. Luckily I had my husband for support and we had his sister, her husband and family to meet us when we finally reached Dunedin, and to give us a roof over our heads until we found our flat – so we were not entirely without direction. We were very lucky to have accommodation until we found our own. It was difficult to find flats in Dunedin in 1954. Even though lots of immigrants were encouraged to come, the accommodation situation was very poor.

We didn't stay in touch with our old shipmates; they were mostly family people and going to different places at the end of the journey. But after we arrived in Dunedin we got a flat in High Street and that became a gathering place for immigrants. There we met people from England, Scotland and Ireland, and many became lifelong friends. Although locals often invited us to come and visit, we soon realised this was a spur-of-the-moment invitation that they did not expect us to take up them up on.

We had no phone in the flat but there was a phone box close by and a little grocery

A child in dress-up with passengers in the background. The peep-toe shoes were fashionable at the time.

shop just down the road. (There were still small grocery shops back then.) We had a cable-car service just outside the door, and were there in 1957 to see the last cable-car service travel down High Street. My daughter attended a primary school just at the top of High Street for a short while before we bought our first little car – a Ford Prefect – and managed to put a small mortgage down on an old house.

My husband had an assured factory job in Shacklock's [Dunedin appliance manufacturer, H E Shacklock, now owned by Fisher & Paykel] but later moved back to driving trolley buses around Dunedin. He was a mechanic originally, but in 1947, a year after he was de-mobbed, he started work driving buses. I met him a couple of years later on the buses as I worked as a bus conductress/clippie. We married in 1952.

I got a job at the Roslyn Woollen Mill. However, my husband died nine years into our new life here, and I was left with a child and a mortgage. With my husband dying, the decision to stay was not made easy, and I had to rely on so many good friends and my husband's family for moral support. I moved into secretarial work, and continued in secretarial/office work up until my retirement at age 60.

The lads found it very strange going into the pubs here and getting their beer poured from hoses – they couldn't believe their eyes. Another early memory that has stayed with me was going into a greengrocers shop owned and operated by Chinese, and seeing some wonderfully big "plums" – I loved plums. But they turned out to be tree tomatoes (now called tamarillos), not plums at all!

I found some luxuries were not available and the styles were a little behind but we caught up eventually in New Zealand. I missed Garibaldi biscuits.

I noticed how much the women actually did in the home – baking, sewing, knitting, etc, and nothing was a bother. Having started her working life as a

Cathie (on the right) holding little Catherine with one of the young women working in the nursery and one of her charges.

domestic servant, as did many young Scottish girls, my mother was very capable. She would sew and knit and cook as much as was possible, but in post-war Scotland it was more convenient to pick up or buy clothes. And due to the lack of room and facilities in our homes back in Scotland – especially where I grew up – it was normal to pop down to the local bakeries to pick up your weekly pies and puddings.

There was a lack of dances and organised events in New Zealand compared to what we were used to, but inter-family socialising here was wonderful. We formed great friendships, and I had a good network of ex-pats and local friends that we always mixed with. So we had lots of parties and beach outings with all the children. Fishing trips and camping were favourite family outings for us. We led a great social and outdoor life.

We found the doctor/health system good, although any Public Health System always has its limitations. My daughter had to get her tonsils/adenoids out quickly at a small private hospital (the Chalet) across the road in High Street, and we had to pay in order to get it done without delay. The calibre and care from the local doctors was excellent. My husband developed lung cancer so we experienced the hospital care system over a long period, and it was as good as it could have been anywhere.

I have no major regrets about coming to New Zealand apart from occasionally being too far from home, especially when my parents were dying. You could not

Catherine in her pram with local children. Curacao.

get back home as easily as you can now. You have to make a life wherever you are! I have one daughter, one grandson and two great-grandsons.

I returned to the UK for my first visit in 1984 to see the family, but just made it in time to see my brother before he died. I went back in 2004 and luckily made it to see my other brother and sister before they died. This was a good call. I have been back once again in 2007 and feel that all ghosts have been laid to rest.

Illustrations acknowledgement

All photographs and other original material were supplied by Catherine (Cathie) Hill and her daughter, Cathy (Catherine) Stevens.

CHAPTER 15

Mae Henderson

Name	Mae Henderson
Ship	TSS *Captain Cook*
Departure date	12 October 1954
Arrival date	17 November 1954
Destination	Unknown until arrival – "a small hospital in New Zealand"
Marital status	Single
Profession	SRN (State Registered Nurse)
Intention	To return after two years

Although I was from a very close family, in 1954 I was tempted by a "bit of an adventure". And, as I said to my family, "it would only be for two years"!

In 1953 while working as a Staff Nurse at Law Hospital, Carluke, Scotland, I saw an advertisement in the *Nursing Mirror* for registered nurses to work in any hospital in New Zealand. A friend decided she would like to apply too. We sent off our applications and after supplying references from our hospital, a police report, a medical report, and a report from the Headmaster of the school where we had completed our education, we were invited to travel to Glasgow to be interviewed by New Zealand officials. They told us they would send for us when they had reviewed all our data. Joy – a few months later we were accepted. We made another trip to Glasgow to be given all details of our future voyage which was to take place on 12 October 1954 [See Appendix 2 for examples of documentation]. Unfortunately, at the last moment my friend announced she was not going and that I should not go either but stay and do as we had intended before seeing the advertisement, which was to specialise in orthopaedics.

I had told everyone I was going, so being stubborn, I decided I would make the journey on my own, not knowing anyone, or anything about New Zealand. At 6.30am on 12 October, heart in mouth and terrified but with a very brave face and accompanied by all my family, I boarded the train in Motherwell going to Clydeside. I bade everyone farewell and walked up the gangway with a very heavy heart, but kept a stiff upper lip.

We sailed, if I remember rightly, about 11am, down the Clyde and out into the Irish Sea where we were hit by the tail end of a hurricane. Boy, did that ship rock – as did my stomach. Fortunately, I managed to stay in one piece; we were later told

Mae Henderson (left) and
Wynn Herview (right).
Curarco. 1954.

the waves had been 40 feet high. There were 1100 passengers on board, a mixture of Scots, English, Irish, Welsh and quite a number of Norwegians who did not speak English. They were befriended by some Glasgow lads who taught them to speak English but with a very broad Scottish accent – quite something to hear. We soon overcame our fears, mastered our sea legs and settled in to enjoy our journey and make new friends, excitedly wondering where we were going to be spending the next two years.

We stopped twice on the trip out, in Curacao for about five hours and Panama for about six or seven hours.

I don't really remember much about the journey other than we spent a lot of

Leaving Glasgow on the River Clyde. View from the TSS *Captain Cook*. 12 October 1954.

time walking the deck, sunbathing and reading. I was very shy on that journey and often wonder what made me get on that ship. I did not participate much – I listened more. I was at the Captain's table for meals during the journey and was invited with the others to afternoon tea in his cabin. His name was Captain Bankier and he had a daughter living in Auckland. For a while after the voyage I kept in touch with two of the girls, Wynn Herview and Alma Loader, but as the years went on we lost contact – we had gone to different areas of New Zealand.

Looking back I don't think I enjoyed the trip very much. I was bored and had never had such a long period of inactivity. I missed my nursing and I was not a sport-loving person – I would rather have my nose in a book.

There were 27 nurses on board. We had been given the choice of the type of hospital, large or small, that we wanted to work in. I opted for a small hospital as Law Hospital where I trained had 1200 beds.

After six weeks we anchored out in Wellington Harbour, and awaited the arrival of the Officials – Customs, Labour Department and Postal. I was apprehensive and very excited. It was great to get a big pile of mail from family and friends, and a letter from the Labour Department telling us where we were going. I was going to Stratford, wherever that was. At this time I had not met many of the other nurses. Our letter told us that we had to meet in A deck lounge at 7.30am where we would be taken by bus to Nursing Headquarters. There we would be spoken to by the Director of Nursing and pay our one pound registration fee so we would be able to start work right away.

Next morning all 27 of us were lined up ready for instructions. The one nurse I was friendly with was standing next to me. Her surname was Anderson and mine was Henderson. Names were called out and we answered "here". Ann's name was called – "here" she answered. Then mine was called, we thought, but unbeknown to us the official had not heard Ann's reply and repeated the Anderson which, in the unfamiliar Kiwi accent, to us sounded like Henderson. We all trotted off down the gangway to the waiting bus taking us into Wellington. On the bus we were asking each other, "Where are you going?" Someone said to me, "Where are you going Mae?" "Oh I am going to a place called Stratford", I said. "Where is that then?" No one knew, but suddenly a voice piped up and said, "Oh there was another nurse going to Stratford but she was told she did not have time to go to HQ as the bus for Stratford was leaving at 10am. You are not supposed to be here. Your registration was going to be done by mail."

Panic! I went up to the front of the bus to the man in charge, and told him what had happened. He was most unconcerned and just said, "Don't worry, she'll be right". Don't worry! He had no idea of my inner turmoil. I actually told him five times that I should not be there and asked him if he could get me back to the ship somehow, but he couldn't have cared less and just kept telling me, "She'll be right". I had never heard that expression before that day.

At 11am we arrived back at the ship. I flew off that bus and ran up the gang plank headed for A deck lounge, and very breathlessly explained to the official who I was and what had happened. Well he swore at me and called me "for all the stupid females" – never in my life have I had a person be so rude to me! He swore blind that he had not called my name. I said he called it after nurse Anderson's name – he quietened down then and apologised, remembering that he had not heard Ann's reply. He explained that there had been a search party out for me and the bus had been delayed and was nearly an hour late in starting its journey north, only ten minutes before I arrived back.

I was ready to stay on that ship and go on the return journey back to Scotland! There were still some passengers on board but most of my friends had gone on their way. I had to go to the dining room at 12.30, have a meal and report back to A deck lounge at 2pm. I did so, and during that time I came into contact with five young men whom I knew slightly. They were going to Wanganui but there had not been enough room on the bus going north to New Plymouth so they had to travel by service bus. They presumed that would be how I would go and said, "Stick with us, you will be fine". I was glad of their company.

I reported back to A deck and was told I was booked on the service bus but my ticket had gone on the other bus, so they had to explain to the driver who I was and why I didn't have a ticket. When the drivers changed at Foxton I had to explain again to that driver when he came around to check our tickets. We boarded the bus, six of us together, but I was told my seat was at the back as the other seats were booked. So there I was – away up at the back and my last link with home at the front of the bus. I felt so lonely.

Leaving Glasgow on the River Clyde. View from the TSS *Captain Cook*. 12 October 1954.

However a nice lady sat beside me and we got talking. When she discovered I had just arrived she was full of information about New Zealand. I did ask her how far it was to Stratford, "Oh not far," she informed me. By our Scottish standards I thought maybe as far as Motherwell was from Edinburgh – not that it was nearly four times that distance! I kept looking at the sign posts expecting to see Stratford at any moment. The roads were fairly winding and some parts unsealed so the journey was much slower than it is today.

We stopped at Foxton for a cuppa and change of driver but no way was I leaving that bus – I would starve first! The lady beside me assured me that the driver would have a drink too, so I agreed to go out to the cafe and was also able to have a conversation with my last links from home. We rejoined the bus and when the new driver came to check our tickets I had to explain my situation once again. "Ah, you're the girl that missed the bus, eh?" I was so embarrassed. So we were once again on our way. The next stop was Wanganui – the boys turned around and waved to me. My lady friend had left the bus at Bulls so there was only another man on the bus. I watched the boys. They were met by two men then I saw them wave to me to come out of the bus. Very reluctantly I went out and there was a gentleman from the Labour Department who had been informed of my situation and came to take me to tea as the bus stayed there for an hour. So I had my first taste of New Zealand fish and chips. He then took me back to the bus and told me he was going to ring the matron at Stratford and tell her I was on the way. It was dark by this time and, unlike in Scotland where they pull the blinds down in the bus and we are well lit up with the driver in his own cabin, here the driver was in the bus with us so all lights were off. The only other man on the bus came

145

and sat beside me. I was very apprehensive about a strange man being so friendly. However, I asked him where he was going and when he said "Stratford", it was the first time I had relaxed on the whole journey.

We eventually arrived there at 9pm and waiting for me were two English nurses, one who was on the ship with me and the other had come on the previous journey of the *Captain Cook*. They took me to the nurses' home and helped me settle in and said they would collect me in the morning as I had to see Matron at 9am. In Matron's office next morning I had to give her all details of my next of kin, etc. When I gave her my parents' address she put her pen down and said, "I used to go to the old Hope Street School". It was lovely that she was from home, although she had been in New Zealand for many years.

So I started work as a nurse at Stratford Hospital, Taranaki, and lived in the nurses' home. In the beginning I relieved the ward sisters until I got used to New Zealand ways. Matron was wonderful to me and all the staff was so welcoming. Pay! I thought I had landed in heaven. I received double the amount that I did at home and worked only eight hours! Previously at home it was 12 hours night duty, 10 hours during the day and paid only for 48 hours. The nurses' home was very comfortable and we were well catered for. I had no restrictions placed on me. In fact, there was a flat attached to the hospital and when it became vacant Matron asked me if I would like to live there where I would be able to entertain friends since I had no home in New Zealand. Of course, you could not take visitors to the nurses' home, especially males. I made so many friends, and when they knew I was on my own the people of Stratford were all wonderful to me and welcomed me into their homes. They were very happy days.

Social activity in New Zealand in the country and farming areas was quite different to the UK but there was always plenty to do. Being staff, we were well taken care off. We had a recreation room at the nurses' home. We played tennis, table tennis and walked for miles – no cars in these days and only a couple of buses going through to New Plymouth each day. We went to the Saturday night dances around the district, to the pictures, and had enjoyable nights in the nurses' home playing cards.

The first six months were a big learning curve. I did not know anything about Maoris or farms and children running round town in their bare feet. I felt so sorry for them and wanted to buy them shoes until someone explained Maoris liked going barefoot like that. In Scotland we would only have gone bare-footed at the beach.

One little Maori boy in the children's ward kept crying for "Mimi". I kept telling him mummy would be there soon and then he wet his bed. I gently told him that was not the thing to do, until one of the other nurses informed me he had been telling me he wanted a MIMI (weewee), not his mummy. Half of the time the nurses could not understand me with my broad Lanarkshire accent [Lanarkshire, Scotland], so I had to consciously modify my way of speaking.

My first holiday after six months was spent with one of the Maori nurses who had time off at the same time and offered to take me around. It would be one of the best holidays I ever had. She took me to Taupo where we stayed with her Aunt and Uncle on their ancestral land. I don't know when he managed to milk his cows, as they seemed to devote all their time to taking me around. We then went to other relations in Rotorua – they put on a big party for me. I can remember sitting on the floor and being enthralled with the most beautiful music and singing which went on for hours. She then took me to her grandparents – her grandfather was related to Princess Te Puia. Once again, I was fascinated by the stories her grandmother related to me of old Maori legends.

Aside from my family, there were not many things I missed. I think the main one was my Yardley's toiletries, so I had plenty sent out to me. Matron used to say, "I can smell Sister Henderson, she is somewhere near". It was a nice smell, thank goodness. It was my trade mark.

Food in New Zealand was so plentiful! I had to stop taking milk in my tea as the milk from those lovely Jersey cows was too creamy for me. Of course, in those days I did not know anything about cows – in fact, I was scared of them. I was very careful not to say, "We don't do that in Scotland" unless someone specifically asked what we did. I did my best to fit in and accept things as they were. I found clothes very expensive, and not the variety we had at home, but food was very plentiful. Cheap lollies were not as nice as at home.

What I missed most was my family, but for 14 years before my mother died, she wrote to me every night before going to bed and Dad posted the letter in the morning on his way to work. The mail did not come so fast in those days and sometimes, depending on what plane they caught, I would have a bundle of six or seven letters at once. My cousins and my aunts and uncles all used to write, so I knew everything that was happening.

I spent eight very happy years in Stratford and made many good friends. It was not a conscious thought to stay in New Zealand – it was something that just happened slowly. I loved being here, loved my work and all the new friends I had made. I think I gained a lot of confidence in life. In 1960 I took six months' leave of absence from the hospital in Stratford and returned to the UK. I knew that would give me enough time to make up my mind where I wanted to live.

My eight years at the hospital ended because I met Russell Wilson in bed! I was sister in charge of the men's ward and had been on days off. My first job back on duty was always to go round my patients and have a little talk to them. I came to a new patient – one look at him and my heart went bump – I did not know what had happened to me. He had injured his back getting on to a tractor, and he was in hospital for six weeks. After discharge he had to come for physiotherapy and he always got his appointment at 10 or thereabouts. He knew I would be in my office having morning tea at that time, so naturally, he would look in, I would offer him a drink, and gradually the nurses who were with me would disappear one by one back to their chores. Slowly we got friendly and then he asked me out to the pictures. Two months later he asked me to marry him and six months later we were married. Russell is a fourth generation New Zealander from Scottish ancestors.

Russ was a shepherd and we worked on a sheep farm in Inglewood until our boss sold the farm and took us (by now we had a son and daughter) to his farm in Hawera. Russell spent all his working life as a shepherd – we loved farming life.

Both children are now married; our son now lives in Christchurch and our daughter in Havelock North. We have seven grandchildren. Our daughter was keen for us to move to Hastings so as to be close to her. We took two years to think about it and decided it would be nice to be here with her and her husband and two boys, so 13 years ago we moved and have never regretted it. We don't see so much of our son's family but text messages are frequent.

It may have been a terrible ordeal of a journey but it all turned out well. I have absolutely no regrets about spending the last 54 years in New Zealand, 46 of those married to Russell.

Illustrations acknowledgement

All photographs and other original material were supplied by Mae Wilson (nee Henderson).

Waiting in the Panama for the first lock to fill with water.

The first lock full of water with the gates starting to open so the ship can move.

Life at home

Life at home was not easy for me, our parents both being Salvation Army. We were expected to follow. We were also expected to set a high example to others. It didn't matter whether we wanted to go to church or not, we were expected to attend three times every Sunday. This caused a lot of stress in our home as many restrictions were placed on us, and particularly on me, being the eldest. At the age of 16 years, I was made a Senior Soldier of the Salvation Army and went into an army uniform. This was not what I wanted. I could see the freedom that other people outside the church had and I wanted the same freedom. But my protests were ignored.

On a Saturday night, I would have to go to a Young People's Youth Group called "Torchbearers". The RSA was directly opposite the Salvation Army where we went for our meeting, and every Saturday night they would have a dance. I would make excuses to go outside and I would go across the road and stand just outside their building listening to the music. Sometimes when the door was opened I would be able to see the folk dancing, and I loved this. I never dared go in though. Of course, Mother always seemed to find out, and I would be in terrible trouble. She was extremely harsh, and I would get far more than just a smack. At this time, Salvationists were not allowed to go to dances or Public Halls of this nature. We were most definitely not allowed to drink or smoke, and we never did.

I thought that it was normal that I be able to socialise with my fellow workmates now that I was working. Unfortunately this was not the case, and unless I was going out to Youth Group or Church activities, I was NOT allowed to go. When I was 17 and a half I climbed out of my front bedroom window one night and went to the movies with another girl from work. Mother was waiting with the poker for me when I got home, and I got a thrashing.

It was only a short time after this that I got home from work one night to find my bags packed and out on the front doorstep. All Mother would say to me was "close the door behind you". I left home.

Away from home

For a few nights, I slept in people's garages, and then a boy that I had met took me to a Catholic Priest's house. The Priest arranged board for me with some Catholic people. When Mother found out that I was living with Catholics, she came and took me home. But it wasn't long before she put me out again.

I tried to visit home many times after this, but the door was always shut in my face and I was told I was wasting my time. I would telephone but Mum would always hang up on me. My Dad was so busy working I don't think he even knew what went on. Mother ruled the home with an iron hand and an unforgiving spirit.

I drifted through the next couple of years, and left Hamilton's Sports Shop to work at Deschler's Hotel where I could also get accommodation. I worked in the kitchen and had a little room out the back. Life was quite lonely.

Those years were the saddest years in my life. I felt as if I had no-one. I missed my family.

By the time I was 20 years of age, I was pregnant and my mother and Church family would have nothing at all to do with me. I was shunned completely. Each Friday night, the Salvation Army band would hold their "Open Air Meeting" on the corner just along from where I worked. I would wait till I knew that they were there, and I would take the mail to post just so I could catch a glimpse of my Dad and any other family members that might be there. Often, my mother would be standing there with my little brother and she would pull him back in close beside her so he would not be allowed to speak to me.

I was told I had brought disgrace and shame on the whole family.

One day I met a lady from the church who we knew well. She told me in no uncertain terms, what a "wicked girl" I was and how I should be ashamed of what I had done to my mother. (Two years later, her son got a church girl pregnant. She was very nice to me after that!)

My Dad was a lot more understanding and found me a little flat, which I moved into with my boyfriend. As we were both under 21 years of age, we applied to the court for permission to get married, but this was declined. My mother would not consent, and on applying for consent my boyfriend found out that the woman he thought was his mother was actually his grandmother; his mother was the person he knew as his sister. She did not want anything to do with him and didn't want the rest of her family to find out she had a child out of wedlock. So we lived together.

My first little girl was born in December 1963, in the Dee Street Maternity Home. I thought she was just beautiful and loved her to bits. I breastfed her for the two weeks while I was there. My boyfriend visited me each day, and on the day I was to be released he was there waiting to take us home to our flat.

I will never forget that day. I dressed my baby in all her new clothes, some that I had saved hard for and bought, and her singlet, matinee jacket, bonnet and booties that I had knitted for her. I wrapped her in her lovely new white shawl and I carried her along to the office to sign the release papers.

But Mother was there with the Social Welfare Officer, and they said I was not allowed to take my baby out. She was taken away. I went back to the Home each day to have my milk expressed and they kept this for her until they found a home for her. I was given pills to dry up my milk but my breasts ached for ages.

I wandered the streets for weeks looking at all the babies I saw and wondered if they could be mine. My heart just ached for her and I couldn't understand why this should be done to me. I was 20 years and five months of age, almost of legal age, which was 21 at that time. The reason given to me was that I had no means of supporting my baby except my boyfriend and the Welfare would not accept this – there were no benefits back then.

I found out through the Social Welfare that my baby had gone to a family that lived in Bluff. So I went there and found her. The family were very good to me and allowed me to stay with them and nurse and care for my baby for a few weeks. However, when she was eight weeks old, she was taken away again by the Social Welfare and I was told it was because I was getting too attached to her. She was moved on somewhere else, and I never found her again.

It wasn't long before my relationship with my boyfriend broke up. He gave me a cheque to go and get some groceries one day. He told me it was his pay cheque so I did this quite openly and took the change back to him. It wasn't long after this that the police took me to the station for questioning and I found out that the cheque had come from a stolen cheque book. I was kept in the police cells for almost a week until my court appearance. Mother was phoned but refused to bail me out so there I stayed. She did send a Bible for me to read though.

My boyfriend ended up going to prison (the Boys Borstal in Invercargill). I was put on probation for a year and was not allowed to associate with him. I never saw him again. I also had to work where instructed. I never did anything else dishonest or got into any of the trouble for the rest of my life.

I was very stressed at this time; I used to cry a lot, mostly missing my baby and the rest of my family. I was very depressed, and I took an overdose of pills and ended up in hospital.

My mother arranged for me to be put into Seacliff [psychiatric hospital], I was placed there under observation for six weeks. They gave me a lot of tests, mental and physical. I think I must have passed them all as years later my Dad told me that they as parents had been brought to the hospital and told that there was nothing at all wrong with me, but had they thought that Mother could be the problem? I wasn't mental, but grieving.

A job was found for me at the Gore Public Hospital working in their children's ward as a Nurse Aid for a few months. Then I went on to the Ranfurly Hospital where I worked in the office.

These early years in New Zealand for me were extremely difficult and I find it very hard to write about, so really have only just touched the surface of all that went on during these years.

I adored my Dad and we would meet on the quiet perhaps for a coffee or lunch outside the home that Mother never knew about. (Mother never had anything more to do with me till after I was married and had my "first" child, in her eyes – my second daughter. She came to visit me in the maternity annexe and took my little girl, showing her off to everyone saying, "This is my very first grandchild".)

From Ranfurly, I came to Oamaru to work on the assembly line at the Regina Sweet Factory. I flatted with three other young girls. One of them had a little girl whom her mother looked after and she took me out to the farm one night for me to meet her. This is where I met my future husband-to-be, her brother, Gordon Robb. I ended up marrying him a couple of years later. He was a poultry farmer. His mother, Charlotte Robb (nee Wilson) was the most wonderful woman. She had married a man 33 years older than herself, who had lost his first wife, Susan

May Douglas, at a young age and left him with three children. Gordon's Mum bought up their three children, along with a further seven children that she had to her husband, Hamilton Robb. She taught me more about being a mother and the meaning of family than I had ever known. No matter what, she stood religiously behind every one of her children and was not only a loyal faithful Mum to her family, but also loyal and faithful to her Lord. She was what I would call a real Christian and showed it in her everyday actions. She took me into her home and I boarded there for a year before marrying Gordon.

Married life

Gordon and I were married in November 1965 in the Presbyterian Church at Maheno, south of Oamaru. We lived on the farm (which in time we purchased), and my mother-in-law moved into the Oamaru Township.

Gordon was born a New Zealander, both parents also New Zealanders, but his grandparents came from Scotland. Gordon and I had five children, a daughter and four sons.

Twenty years after my first daughter was born, she found me and got in touch. We have developed a relationship to the point that now she is just one of the family. She had a wonderful upbringing with very good adoptive parents; her adoptive Mum is now deceased, but her Dad is still alive.

Almost 20 years after our marriage we purchased another poultry farm, only a few metres from where we live and we are still living there. My husband Gordon has resided in the same area for the 65 years of his life. From my six children we have 19 grandchildren and three great-grandchildren.

Although we still [in 2008] live on our farm, the poultry side of the business is now finished and we just run a few beef cattle, enough to keep my husband occupied during the day. With six of us at home and others always coming and going my days seem to be pretty full.

Since I married I have been a full-time homemaker and have not gone out to work. I have brought up my five children from my marriage, also have helped in raising my eldest granddaughter and cared for other grandchildren at different times. I am continuing with child care with my youngest son's two children. I keep my hand in with a small amount of book and paperwork, accounts, etc each month, and GST to do every second month.

In my earlier years I had some regrets about coming to New Zealand. When my grandparents one by one passed away we were unable even to go back for the funerals. I realised I would never see them again and that was hard to bear. Since then a lot of my aunts and uncles and cousins have also died. In the last few years my Dad's only living two brothers and their wives have visited us and it was an amazing feeling. After 50 years I still felt so close to them and didn't want them to go home again. I would have loved to have kept them here.

Even though I have married and have my own family now, I have always felt drawn to Coventry over the years and a real need to find out what I could about my extended family. I have felt the loss of my extended family to be a huge gap in my life; but I have never had any regrets about remaining and living in New Zealand.

I have never been back to the UK and probably in the family situation I am in now, I will never be able to go although I would dearly love to. I know that things would not be the same as I remember them but it would be nice to see my cousins and the rest of my family that is still alive.

My mother died in 1988 and my father died in 2004, sixteen years later.

I do still miss some things from England: Battenberg cake! This was my favourite cake in England and we cannot get it here – I have asked at shops around the different places I have been and most of them don't even know what Battenberg cake is. Also long gone are the long finger-shaped mini ice-blocks that we had as children; the penny's worth of broken biscuits we used to be able to buy; and sherbet that we used to get in a triangular white paper bag with a straw that we used to suck through – it was fizzy and sometimes would tickle our noses.

I do miss the little squirrels. We would walk through the woods each day to school in Coventry and they would often throw acorns down at us then scurry back up the tree. I miss the robins in the winter months with their brightly coloured red breasts. This is wildlife that we do not see here in New Zealand.

And since being in New Zealand, I have never seen the Punch and Judy shows that we often saw in England.

However, I believe I have a wonderful home and life here in New Zealand, certainly compared to what my cousins have in England, so I guess Dad did give us the opportunity to have a better life when we came to New Zealand.

CHAPTER 17

Rosemary Thompson

Name	Edith Rosemary Thompson (Rosemary)
Ship	SS *Captain Hobson*
Departure date	28 December 1956
Arrival date	11 February 1957
Destination	North Island
Marital status	Engaged (changed ships from the TSS *Captain Cook* to travel with her future husband whom she had met in England July 1956)
Profession	Office worker
Intention	Depended on how things went

Rosemary and her fiancé Jim, who both worked as civilians at the Air Ministry in Carlisle, didn't see much of a future in the UK. Jim had seen quite a bit of the world as he had been in the RAF since he was 16 and had only been out of the Forces for two years; Rosemary had not seen any of it and had itchy feet. Although Rosemary was sad at leaving the safe haven of her family, overall she felt ready for an adventure. They also knew that they always had the option of coming back after two years if it didn't work out.

Rosemary's parents had planned to come out to New Zealand after the First World War, but her Grandma had thrown a sickie and Rosemary's mother felt she should stay to care for her. As it turned out, her grandmother lived until 1944 when she passed away at the age of 80. Rosemary's parents eventually came out to New Zealand for a visit in 1964, following a trip that Rosemary made back home in 1963.

Aside from what she had been told by a teacher at her primary school, who, for some unknown reason, talked a lot about the Canterbury Plains, Rosemary knew little about New Zealand. Some of the information she gained when she was interviewed turned out to be untrue, in particular the impression that in New Zealand one wore light clothing all year around. Fifty years later Rosemary still regrets leaving her lovely Moreland sheepskin-lined boots in the false belief that she wouldn't need them.

At the time, Rosemary thought the immigration authorities must have been anxious to get as many young folk as they could in a short time, as the paperwork flew through the system. Required was proof of a clean bill of health (including an X-Ray), a smallpox vaccination and a Document of Identity. It seemed that provided you were 'sound in mind and limb' and were not illiterate, you passed muster. On 20 March 1956 Rosemary's letter of application was being considered, on 28 June she was interviewed, 29 June she was given a medical,

Rosemary and Jim. Panama. 1957.

30 June an X-ray, and on 18 July her acceptance papers and other information arrived for sailing on the TSS *Captain Cook* on 2 October 1956. By this time Rosemary was a number – 181038 c/o Labour Department, Draft # 63, PO Box, Wellington. However, Jim had not heard from them, so he went down to London for an interview and became number 181405. Jim was scheduled to sail on the SS *Captain Hobson* but Rosemary was able to change berths so she and Jim could sail out together.

This chapter begins with the two initial letters written by Rosemary to her parents back in England. The first letter of 28 pages was written on the trip out to New Zealand, while the second of 18 pages was written shortly after arrival. The originals are on small pages and are rather frail as Rosemary's mother passed them around the locals like "NAAFI sandwiches … (two slices of bread with nothing in the middle)". Rosemary commented, "I suppose in those days someone breaking out of the mould was newsworthy. I was a celebrity!"

The chapter concludes with Rosemary's more recent comments on the experience in which, as she says, she mentions the less pleasant matters, the things one leaves out of letters to parents.

[Letter from Rosemary to her parents. Dated 19 January 1957, written on the SS *Captain Hobson*]

> Dear Mum, Daddy and Everyone,
> I got your letter at Cristobal also one from Auntie Edith. It certainly is nice to get some letters; I'm looking forward to Wellington and some mail and newspapers. If Tina misses me, I miss her – it seems funny not to see her when I wake up. Whose bed does she sleep on now?
> There is a lot to tell you so I'd better try to get it all in order. This won't get posted

28

when we first saw N.Z. it does seem hard to believe we have really arrived. After coming along the North Island Coast all this morning we will soon be entering Cook Strait that separates the North & South Islands. Well I've some last minute ironing to do & my 'pecking' as Bill calls it.
Cheerio for now love Jim & Rosies.
    Dear Mum & Daddy.
    I've so much to tell you I had better start another letter or I'll never get this in the envelope.
    Thanks for your letters, I got one also from Mrs Jefferson, wasn't it kind of her to write, I know the woman she means although I've never spoken to her myself.
    See you later alligator.
        Rosies x Jim x

27

Dear Mum & Daddy   1.30pm.
    Well we've arrived at the 'Land of the Long White Cloud'.
    The weather now is beautiful, the sea is much calmer & we can see the rocky coastline of our adopted country, lets hope its everything we wish. We saw land first thing after breakfast, it certainly looks good after 23 days of water, although we were met by the first of the albatros' two days ago & now there are dozens of them gliding so gracefully around the ship, There have been sharks & a whale around this morning anything is a distraction from the never ending waves, someone has only to shout sharks & everyone dives to the rails & starts peering into the sea. Even Jim felt a bit excited

The last two pages of Rosemary's first letter.

until I get to Wellington so I may stop and start as I remember things that will interest you.

I had better start at the beginning of my journey. Well the gales did blow themselves out on us; for ten days we had high winds and high seas, but I'm not too bad a sailor when I compared myself with some of the passengers – I only missed two meals, while some didn't appear at all the first week. The crew told us we would be in sunshine in four days, but it was ten days before we got any good weather. Still, we've made up for it since. All I'd like to do now is to nip home and make everyone jealous of my nice tan. (Jim's just bent over my shoulder and said "plus the peeling", but I haven't done much of that in comparison to some.) It's so lovely to have all this sunshine, it's hard to realise how strong it is compared with home. It has been rather a dull day today, very hot but rather sultry. This morning we saw dozens of porpoises and flying fish and blue shiny fish jumping out of the water, which has been as calm as a mill pond today.

At first some of the kids had measles and the rumours went round that we wouldn't be able to go ashore at Curacao but there was no truth in it, luckily, although Willemstad the capital is not so very exciting [the Historic Area of Willemstad, the inner city, and harbour at Curacao are now a World Heritage Site and major

SS *Captain Hobson.*

tourist attraction] – very picturesque if one doesn't look too long at the dreadful hovels some of the people live in.

The population is mainly coloured – several shades and about 40 different nationalities. The remainder are Dutch, the two languages being Dutch and the native tongue which is a mixture of nearly everything – Spanish, Dutch, French – in fact, the bits and pieces of every nation that has occupied them in the past plus American slang which they picked up from the Yanks who looked after the island for Holland during the war.

Studebaker typical of the large American cars in Curacao with "the dreadful hovels" in the background.

Entering Curacao. The remains of some of the old forts built by the Dutch to protect the harbour are visible.

For a place not much bigger than the Isle of Man it is extremely rich, a fact which is only too apparent when one sees the fantastic price of things.

Water is bought by the pint as we buy milk at home. I believe it's somewhere in the region of 1/- per pint as all the drinking water has to be distilled from seawater. The one cheering thing, petrol is only 1/8 per gallon and all the cars are American, the sort they buy by the yard [because they were so big]. Add this to the fact that they never drive less than 70mph and the streets are so narrow that if one of these rainbow-hued monsters comes tearing up, such unimportant obstacles as people dive into the nearest shop doorway.

I got up at 4am on Monday 14 January to see us enter Curacao. It was really beautiful with a full moon shining across the water and the bright harbour lights and the outline of the hills in the distance. My impression of Willemstad was that it is very quaint, most of the buildings being 17th century Dutch architecture, but rather shabby. There is a pontoon bridge over the harbour that has to be opened to let the ship berth. It floats on about 15 boats and swings almost at water level from one side, not like most of the bridges at home that divide in the middle and are high above the water. This contraption is only possible because there is no tide; at least, only about one inch.

What a smell there is to greet you; as soon as we got near the island we could smell it. It comes from the oil refinery, Esso and Shell oil – that will explain its wealth – as it is the nearest place to South America with harbours large enough for the tankers to come in. Everyone, even those who live in the hovels, have cars. It seems funny to see places that look as if they should have fallen down long ago with a car parked outside.

The fruit market consists of small sailing vessels with their prows sticking over the wharf and all their wares set out on the prow of the boat and on orange boxes,

Photo courtesy of Phyllis Young

Pontoon Bridge.

Pontoon Bridge floating on boats. The pontoon bridge is still a tourist attraction today.

Market stalls on small sailing vessels.

anything from fish and fruit to queer things that the natives chew and smoke or do some weird and wonderful thing with.

So much for our day at Curacao, I'll tell you more about coming through the Panama Canal, Balboa and Panama City later. I must go and get changed now for dinner – must be decent even on an emigrant boat. Cheerio for now.

[Sunday 20 January 1957 7am]

Good morning! It really is a good one. I'm still in bed but the sunshine is streaming through the porthole and it's oh so hot. It was rather cooler last night. It's supposed to indicate hurricanes when it's cool so near the equator, so we'll have to keep our fingers crossed. To you at home it will be 1pm so you will have had your lunch. Maybe it's a mild attack of home sickness, but we all find ourselves reckoning up the time and what our folks will be doing at home.

The ship was running short of water before we arrived at Curacao so they started turning it off during the day, but we took it on at Balboa. We couldn't take water on at Curacao owing to the shortage of it, but we did fill up with oil, to the tune of £16,000 worth.

Now for Panama, which I will remember long after I've forgotten Curacao. We arrived at Cristobal on the Atlantic end of the Canal at 2am and anchored to await the pilot and the mail. We entered the Canal at 7am. I took lots of photos so if any of them turn out okay, I'll send you some so you can see for yourselves. We saw the

The Gaillard Cut, also known as the Culebra Cut, is 8 miles long, 160 yards wide and 45 feet deep.

commencement of the original French canal on our starboard side (I even know left from right now) which is a very narrow channel compared with the present one. We then entered the first of the Gatun locks to lift us up to the second, then up again into the channel that leads into Gatun Lake, a large freshwater lake surrounded by jungle and dotted with wee jungle-covered islands. All there is to see all around and either side of the canal are dense green hills, all shades of green from nearly black to real metallic shades.

Once through the lake we entered the narrowest part, and then down from more locks. By this time we were in the Pacific where there is a tide. It seems funny that all the water is connected yet there is no tide at Curacao. Along the Canal is a plaque to the 4000 who lost their lives [the number was closer to 25,000] during the several, successful and

Panama Canal. The memorial to those who lost their lives building it can be seen on the hillside.

168

YMCA. Balbao.

unsuccessful, attempts to make a waterway through what must have looked like impenetrable jungle and swamp.

Arriving at Balboa at 3pm we went ashore. There isn't much at Balboa itself, only the YMCA where we couldn't buy anything (even if we'd had many dollars), only cards and ices etc. There was a swimming pool which we made good use of later in the evening. All the worry we had over money before we left home and it's easy enough to get pounds changed to dollars. They were very helpful in the YMCA and told us where of interest to go in Panama. From there we got one of those ramshackle buses into the city. They just about hold together, that's all; the speed they go around corners one would expect them to disintegrate altogether. Some of them are all decorated up inside with gaily-coloured raffia tied round things and fancy tassels all over the dashboard and the backs of the seats, which are invariably bursting out all over. Maybe all this tying-up with raffia had another purpose besides being decorative, I don't know!

They seem to charge what they like according to how big a sucker you look; we just gave them 10 cents and got off. If we were to ask them how much it would start at 50 cents and we'd argue down from there. There were eight of us together so we made the most of it. When we got into Panama we got a taxi. Billie our driver took us in one car and the rest followed on behind in another of these half-mile long cars. We really did see the sights: the university, the Governor's house, the Golden Altar and lots more. We stopped at the fruit market where the boys bought some bananas, a great bunch of them that weighed about half a hundredweight for 75c, tangerines, grapefruit and pineapples, so we've been on a fruit diet ever since.

A great bunch of bananas bought from the fruit market.

We then went to El Panama, the most modern hotel in the world, or so it says. It certainly is wonderful; a Yankee skyscraper type, all air-conditioned. So nothing daunted, we went in to have a look-see and ended up by making pigs of ourselves. Beautiful ice cream and lemon meringue concoctions; it was a good change after the food on the boat. Not that there is any cause for complaint as it's good and well cooked but it gets rather monotonous, and it's nice to have something that we wouldn't get on the boat, even if it does make for a sore tummy afterward.

El Panama Hotel. Panama.

Dessert menu. El Panama Hotel.

[30 January 1957]

What a delay, I've almost forgotten the tale and where I was up to. I think we were still in Panama.

We went back into Panama City in the evening and back to El Panama. What a wonderful view of the city we got from the top. After wandering around all the luxurious shops in the hotel we ended up in the casino, but the stakes were too high for our meagre dollars. We just lost a few dimes in the machines and left the roulette to the wealthy. We stayed there about a quarter of an hour and then came down into the candlelight and soft music of the Palm Court, where we sat, talked, danced and drank long cool cocktails until 1am. You should have seen the elaborate wine list headed "Tropical Tempters" and a picture of each served up in whole pineapples and coconuts.

Front of Tropical Tempters Cocktail card. El Panama Hotel.

Tropical Tempters Cocktail card. El Panama Hotel.

Crossing the Line
Ceremony.

Top: Judgment. King
Neptune looks on.

Below: The defendants
in the pool.

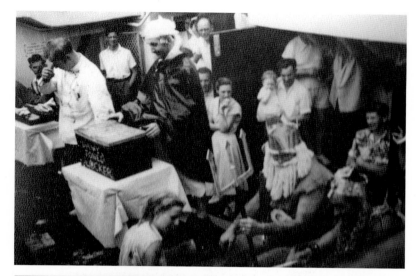

Even the Damas (Ladies) were luxurious pale green toilets, even to the paper and
an attendant to dry my hands for me.

We all wanted to see as much as we could so we went into another place but it was
a real dive. After 10 minutes we'd had enough so we dived out again and went for
a stroll down town and finished up on hamburgers and coffee. We then made our
reluctant way towards a taxi and the boat but no one felt like sleeping, so we took
a walk around Balboa and finally arrived on board about 5am very tired, with
memories of a wonderful day and night. It was a really marvellous night with stars
that looked like diamonds and the full moon hanging like a lantern in the palm
trees. It was hard to imagine how cold it would be at home.

This old tub sailed again at 11am January 18, but not before we'd been back in Panama for a few hours, to collect one or two souvenirs.

Our next bit of excitement was the ceremony when we crossed the line. We actually crossed the equator on January 20 but the ceremony wasn't held until January 22. The crew rigged a canvas pool up on deck and after selecting 18 victims, two of them crew, and neither of us two I'm glad to say, all the messy ceremony began. I hope the snaps of it I took come out because some of them were just taken behind the heads of people. We all got the benefit of flying soot, soap powder, water and "off" kippers, but at least we weren't smothered in it like the "defendants" who were accused of all sorts from playing the bagpipes to plotting the ship's course so that according to them we should be somewhere in Hyde Park. One girl was found guilty of misuse of the ship's electricity supply by burning herself on the iron.

[5 January 1957]

Well I'm slowly catching up on events; we are back in time now 10½ hours from England and we cross the International Date Line between Thursday night and Saturday so we won't have any Friday. That makes us 12 hours in front of you at home, so for as long as we are on this side we'll be waking up when you are sleeping. I hope you can sort that lot out.

On Wednesday 30 we visited Pitcairn Island – at least we anchored offshore for about three hours in the afternoon. An emerald isle in a setting of blue sea, blue skies and sunshine, a real paradise for the 140 inhabitants who are nearly all descendants of the Bounty mutineers and who still retain the names of Christian and Fletcher, etc.

These happy bronzed people came out from the island in small boats, with fruit, and souvenirs, all of them home-made things like baskets, flying fish, tortoises

Pitcairn Island.

Pitcairn Islanders rowing out to the SS *Hobson*.

and birds carved out of wood – all carved with the name of the person who made them. We bought a basket and a flying fish; goodness knows where it's going to get packed away but we'll find room somewhere.

Of course, we had to have a go at all the different fruits. Paw-paw is awful, at least it smells so, and the taste is not so hot. They are like melons to look at only more pear-shaped. Then there were passion-fruit about the size of a plum but with a shell and it's the seeds inside that are eaten, they're nice. What else now? Coconuts fresh with plenty of milk but not much nut, mango that are unlike anything at home but are an acquired taste; I quite like them. Best of all, the pineapples; the small ones are the best, they really are out of this world. Enough of the gourmet for now. After this short spell of excitement, these barefoot islanders bade us goodbye with a song, to await the *Corinthian* which calls there a few days after us and also takes our mail off Pitcairn. I hope you keep that letter for the stamps, as well as the other ones with the Panama and Curacao stamps on, Mum.

I don't think anyone on this boat will be sorry to leave it and start work; the boredom of having nothing to do and all day to do it in is just about getting everyone's nerves to breaking point. If ever I come home it will be on a boat a bit bigger than 9000 tons and it will have everything, swimming pool and a decent library. One person who had to pay was the padre's wife. Fancy paying £135 to be on this boat when that same money could get you a passage on one of the big boats.

All this discontent that seems to have infected everyone will soon be forgotten by Sunday when we arrive in Wellington, although we will have to stay in the harbour until Monday when we disembark at last. Jackie, in the same cabin as me, says that she's going to swim ashore.

I expect when we all talk about this trip in years to come we'll have forgotten all the bad bits and remember the good times. It's a good job memories are like that or we'd be harbouring grudges all our life.

Rosemary and friends,
beautifully dressed, at Panama.
Rosemary is on the right.

[In 2008 Rosemary described the lack of luxuries on the *Hobson*. "There was no entertainment other than what we made ourselves. The officers were mostly Scots and a few of them played the accordion for dancing, and were very patient and generous with their time for a bunch of entertainment-starved youngsters. I do not recollect much in the way of alcoholic drinks or boozing – but then we did not have a lot of money to splash around on it on anyway.

"We tried to learn sign language and Morse code and played endless card games. I taught a guy to crochet a settee chair-back but all he had was army string, so it turned out HUGE. The other way of passing the time was in little romances, although with a lot of passengers on a smallish ship privacy was at a premium. The events that featured as part of the daily routine were mealtimes, and waiting for a certain Sheila to finish ironing her damn knickers so I could iron my four yards of Horrockses cotton that was mandatory for any self-respecting young lady's dress in the 50s.

"It was wonderful, all that lovely warmth and sunshine. And I, having been a wartime kid, had never experienced an adventure quite like it before".]

We are all waiting now to know whereabouts in New Zealand we will be sent as no-one really knows who have been nominated. We just hope it will be where we want, Hamilton in our case.

Practically all the kids have now had measles so that's one thing less for them to get. Every day one or two went missing and emerged ten days later with the remains of their spots. The only good thing is that it helps keep some of the 120 "little dears" out of action for a bit.

Programme for "horse races" on the SS *Captain Hobson*.

```
s.s. CAPTAIN HOBSON                            23rd. JANUARY, 1957
              EQUATORIAL        MEETING
       OF THE HOBSON HORSE RACING ASSOCIATION Inc.

 FIRST RACE       THE  PACIFIC  PRANCE           (Over 2 miles
  1. BREAKFAST                (by Dash out of Bed)
  2. EMBARRASSMENT            (by Curtain out of Place)
  3. ENCHANTED EVENING        (by Boat Deck out of Sight)
  4. FLATULENCE               (by Tummy out of Order)
  5. NUISANCE                 (by Children out of Bounds)
  6. PEACE AT LAST            (by Loudspeaker out of Commission)

 SECOND RACE      THE  GALAPAGOS  GALLOP          (7 furlongs)
  1. BOAT DECK                (by Eleven O'Clock out of Bounds)
  2. UNEASY MOTION            (by Ship out of Glasgow)
  3. DRIVEN                   (by Night Patrol out of Lounge)
  4. CRICK                    (by Neck out of Joint)
  5. DAZZLED                  (by Beach Shirt out of Panama)
  6. STONEY BROKE             (by Syndicate out of Luck)

 THIRD RACE       THE  SOUTH PACIFIC  STEEPLECHASE   (Hurdles)
  1. LOVELY LADY              (by Max out of Factor)
  2. PRETTY FILLY             (by Rum & Coke out of Focus)
  3. SCOTCH REEL              (by Wee Heufs out of Forbidden Bottle)
  4. HOPEFUL MAIDEN           (by Yank out of Panama)
  5. SWINDLE                  (by Purser out of Cash)
  6. NEVER SAY DIE            (by Always out of Luck)

 FOURTH RACE      THE  HUMBOLDT  HANDICAP       (Last horse wins
  1. DOUBTFUL DELIGHT         (by Bagpipes out of Tune)
  2. TRU-FORM                 (by Foundation out of Elastic)
  3. STUFFY CABIN             (by Ventilation out of Order)
  4. TATTERED REPUTATION      (by Gossip out of Ironing Room)
  5. IRON TONIC               (by Water out of Ship's Tank)
  6. NOCTURNE                 (by Stealth out of Cabin)

                    R U L E S
                    ::::::::::
  A. The Hobson Race Course does not come under the jurisdiction of
     the Jockey Club or National Hunt Committee.  We make up our rules
     as we go along.
  B. The decision of the Judges is final.(Even when they are wrong)
  C. Officials and Jockeys may use the Tote.(If they can afford it.)
  D. Jockeys will be appointed for each race.  You are respectfully
     requested not to offer bribes to officials or jockeys. (they
     might accept.)
  E. Feeding the horses (and jockeys) is not allowed while racing is
     in progress.
  F. Beware of pickpockets, touts, welshers, bookmakers and all the
     officials.
  G. Count your change before leaving the Tote.(You may be lucky
     enough to get the correct amount.)
  H. Neither the Management, not the Ministry of Transport & Civil
     Aviation, New Zealand Government, Henderson Line and Shaw Savill
     Line will be responsible for any injuries incurred through horses
     kicking or biting spectators or jockeys.

 TOTALISATOR    This will operate on the Pari-Mutuel System (same
                as at Ascot.  Tickets - 3d. each.  Please ask for
                tickets by number and not by horse's name.  Winners
                will be paid out after each race.
```

[6 January 1957 6.30am]

Good morning. I'm here with my "early" morning cuppa, wondering what else there is to tell you. I think there are only bits and pieces that I've forgotten. Just after we left Panama someone was supposed to have fallen overboard and the ship turned back and lost an hour sailing time all for nothing – it was just another rumour. If there really had been someone over the side they would have had a job to find them in the dark. There was also someone taken off ill at Curacao. He's had an operation and will be coming to New Zealand on another ship.

We are getting our disembarkation papers today so maybe we'll know where we're going, I hope. It's nearly as bad as waiting to know our sailing date at first. We're also having a trial disembarkation just to iron a bit of the chaos out of Monday.

I think I'll get up now as it's awfully stuffy down here, because the portholes are shut on account of the spray. It's a choice between being hot and getting soaked. Looking through our porthole now is like looking through the window of a Bendix washing machine, all foamy.

Someone was saying yesterday that we were the only ship to leave Glasgow during that spell of bad weather, as all the others were called back; maybe they thought that it didn't matter so much about us. Anyway, we went 80 miles off course to try to avoid the worst of the storm.

Well I'd better get up now and shake a leg.

[Sunday 10 February 1957]

This is the last full day on the boat, we are supposed to arrive in Wellington harbour at 3pm but I think it will be later than that as we have lost some time these last two days, on account of the rough seas. It has been practically as rocky as when we first set out from Glasgow and this old boat is creaking and groaning like a sailing ship.

There is another liner to come in just after us, but if it overtakes us in the night it beats us to Wellington anchorage so it may be Tuesday before we dock. We're all keeping our fingers crossed and hoping that we get in before the big ship and will be able to leave the boat on Monday.

We had our practice disembarkation on Thursday, but they only gave us our disembarkation papers and customs forms, so we're still waiting to know where we will be sent. When the port officials and Customs and Immigration people come on board with the pilot we'll all be put out of our misery and know what we are going to and where we are going. The farewell dance was held last night – if you could call it a dance when it took us all our time to stand on our feet – but we enjoyed it nevertheless and some of the fancy dresses were really good.

Well Mum, I had better finish here and I'll tell you more when we've all finished all the palaver and form filling and we're on our way to out destination.

[1.30pm]

Dear Mum and Daddy,

Well we've arrived at the Land of the Long White Cloud. The weather now is beautiful, the sea is much calmer and we can see the rocky coastline of our adopted country. Let's hope it's everything we wish. We saw land first thing after breakfast; it certainly looks good after 23 days of water, although we were met by the first of the albatrosses two days ago and now there are dozens of them gliding so gracefully around the ship. There have been sharks and a whale around this morning. Anything is a distraction from the never-ending waves; someone has only to shout "sharks" and everyone dives to the rails and starts peering into the sea. Even Jim felt a bit excited when we first saw New Zealand. It does seem hard to believe we have really arrived. After coming along the North Island coast all this morning we will soon be entering Cook Strait that separates the North and South Islands. We've some last minute ironing to do and my "packing" as Bill calls it.

Cheerio for now love Jim and Rosies.

Dear Mum and Daddy,

I've so much to tell you, I had better start another letter or I'll never get this in the envelope.

See you later alligator

Rosies and Jim

[Letter written later on 10 February 1957 from Wellington Harbour]

My Dear Mum and Daddy,

Well this is my last night in a bunk on the *Captain Hobson*. Even though she is an old tub she's seen us all safely for 12,000 miles through fair weather and foul. We saw an awful lot of New Zealand before we got to Wellington, coming down the North Island coast. It is very rugged-like, real sandstone cliffs and sandy bays; they certainly are the sort of hills that I like, wild and woolly; the hills behind the bare rock cliffs are all thickly wooded. It was all so grand and so different from what I imagined. The pilot came aboard at 5pm and we watched the harbour anchorage about 6.30, and by 7.30 the immigration and customs officials, who had come aboard, had finished with us all and we knew where we were going and what we're going to do.

Jim and I are both stopping in Wellington and are both in hostels at Trentham about 50 minutes from Wellington itself. I am going to work at "His Masters Voice". Maybe I'll have to look after the wee dog who sits on top of the gramophone! I leave the boat at 9.20am tomorrow along with Barbara who shares my cabin; we are both going to Trentham so we should be fine. I would have liked to be further north but we're together and Jim and I are too glad of that to worry much where we're sent. You have heard me speak of Terry (Teresa for short)? Well, she and her sister Shealah were to be parted, but I think they went to the liaison officers and they are now both going to be in Wellington, so it won't seem altogether like a city of strangers. Jackie, the German girl in this cabin who is joining her brother, will also be in Wellington! We've been looking at a street map of "this fair city" and Jackie and Barbara are working in adjoining streets in the town, I'll have to see where Wakefield Street is, as that's where I'll be working. Margaret, the other girl in this cabin, is going to Christchurch in the South Island.

I'm dying to see Joan [pen-pal whom Rosemary had never met until Rosemary and Jim's wedding day]; I do wish we were a bit nearer Tauranga. She will know we've arrived anyhow, as they give out all the ships and times of arrival on the radio.

Oh Mum, I wish I could send you some of this wonderful weather. I'm sat here in my bunk at 2am Monday with the porthole open and the light shining through from the houses perched up the hills surrounding this beautiful harbour. It's comfortably warm now, not so horribly hot like it was in the tropics when it was too hot to sleep. Not that I feel like sleeping now, I don't, but I suppose if I hope to get up for breakfast I better get some sleep.

Goodnight both, all our best.

Love Rosies and Jim

[23 February 1957]

Dear Mum and Daddy,

Well love, a lot has happened since the 11th Feb when we landed. I started work on the 13th at HMV. The work isn't too bad but the pay isn't much when it costs me 15/- per week to get to work. The pay to start was £7.6.0 with £1 bonus if I wasn't later than 10 minutes during the week. Anyway, I've got myself another job. I don't know whether I'll like it but I start at £11. They wanted someone experienced, but Cheeky went in and got the job so he said he'd give me £11 (which is 10/- less than the rate for the job) to learn, plus bonuses and as much overtime as I like. This job is in a place making tin cans. I didn't tell him that I hadn't the vaguest idea about it but they're glad to get workers.

I had to go to the Emigration Department to see if I could change, so I gave my notice in yesterday at HMV and I'll be up to see the Labour Department again on Monday to get it all fixed. I must say it's a bit like being on probation, them knowing all your business and having to go to them before I can change my job, but they're very nice about it.

Jim and I are in this hostel about 18 miles from Wellington and have to be up and at the station at 5 to 7 in the morning. The food is army style. We're roughing it, but I don't suppose it will do us any harm.

One thing, we don't starve, even if we don't like the food here. I have a pint of milk here every night and one at work at dinnertime and tons of fresh fruit. They sell apples 10lb at a time for 6/6 straight off the trees and in polythene bags. Everything to do with food (except maybe at the camp here) is beautifully clean and you can get lovely salads in all the milk bars. There aren't usually any dives as we know them at home – all the cafes and food shops are spotless, and most of the green-grocers are kept by Chinese.

Housing is terrifically dear but there is a man who lives at Heretaunga and travels on the same train as Jim and me in the morning and he says that they (he and his wife) know an elderly couple who are going to live at Rotorua sometime and he'll see what he can do about us renting their place, so we are keeping our fingers crossed. He said the rent may be about 30-odd bob a week. Places like that are advertised at about £8 up to £15 a week so two couples have to share a place like that. Being here at Upper Hutt is a long way from town, and if we did get this place I should get a job somewhere nearer home.

When anyone gets overtime at home they're lucky; here when you work overtime you get asked if you're "hungry", which means "mean" here. The man who told us about this place is as Yorkshire as the dales – he's from Leeds and has been here 30 years. He works for the New Zealand film unit and has asked Jim and me up to his house to see some pictures sometime.

In the camp it's like a league of nations: New Zealand police and army, and English, Irish, Scottish, Welsh, Samoans, Hungarians, Germans, Belgians and Dutch. I'm sharing a room with Barbara who was with me on the boat; she's away this weekend with another girl who was on the boat, who is living with her married sister at Woburn a few miles away.

Vera, a woman I work with, asked Jim and me up to her place at Oriental Bay last Saturday and we had a lovely time. Her flat is perched up on a hill overlooking the harbour. Vera and her husband have been out here nine years and are also from Yorkshire. She was going home this year for a visit but her mother died, so she sent for her father and he's been here since November and is very happy.

She's 40-ish I would say, and I think she takes it on herself to mother English couples because she tells us about two more couples who used to live here in Wellington and were great friends, but they've both gone to live in Nelson.

Last Saturday Vera and Ted took us all round in the car and what beautiful views there are from the top of the hills. Saturday and Sunday are all one here and everyone goes on picnics or barbecues down to the rivers or beaches. Last Saturday from Vera's verandah we were watching the four-man skiffs racing in the harbour and the big boats coming in and out. The ferry goes to Christchurch once a day. It's a beautiful boat, a bit bigger than the *Hobson*. I believe that you can get a cabin on it and there is dancing all night if you feel energetic.

Most of the entertainment here is outdoors, water skiing and boating and swimming.

There is a big nine-day shoot up here at Trentham, up on the hills. I think they go after the wild goats. There is also a big show here yesterday and today. Vera and Ted came down for me in the car this morning to go to it, but I want to do some washing and wash my hair. Jim's working today and we are going to the pictures tonight and are going to stop at Vera's overnight, so we'll be off somewhere on a picnic tomorrow.

Jim bought a radio from a chap he works with but I'm afraid he hasn't had any use from it as Babs and I have it in our room. They don't go in for kettles out here much, it's usually jugs with an element in so we've got one and we'll have a cuppa at night.

Jim started to have the cut lunches that they put up here but he needed some binoculars to see what was in them so I put them up now. Electrical stuff is very dear, our jug was going on for £3 but as Babs works at the store where we got it, we got 10/- knocked off. Babs bought a Murphy Richards iron which was over £3. I can send you some money and a list of things you can bring when you come out, things like blankets. There is wonderful variety in the shops but most things are dearer than home, though food is cheaper. Here all the people are well dressed. I've never seen so many girls in pretty dresses with tons of petticoats underneath. To buy dresses would be expensive but as most of the girls sew and material isn't any more expensive than at home (at least, not enough to mention), they can afford to look nice. You'd have to look a long time to find anyone who looks really poverty stricken.

It doesn't seem much good for Jim and me to stop here longer than we can help; we'd be far better off married if we got some place reasonable. What most people do is try to get some place then travel as much around New Zealand as they can, which for most people is all over, then pick a place that they would like to live and after two or three years they can afford to buy a section and build a house.

You know I could have cried when I unpacked that wooden box. You know that pretty bowl that you brought back from Penton? Well it's bust. I don't think I'll be able to mend it as it's chipped as well as broken – to think how well it was packed. One fruit dish and that Teddy coronation mug went for a burton, and my brass clock is all green and corroded [it was later cleaned up and went for years]. My sewing machine is ok though, I'm glad to say. Also bust were a couple of plates, so maybe I haven't done too badly.

It's the start of winter here, so they say they should have England's winter, and it rained all day yesterday which is good, as Wellington has only had about two or three days rain since November and is looking rather parched. But the sun is shining in a blue sky again today; it really does your heart good.

Daddy wants to stick it out till he's got a good pension when he's 65 then get the first boat to the Land of the Long White Cloud and take a chance on being called a Pommy. Even though it's a bit rough and ready here, we've no regrets, Jim and I – in fact, everyone – has found a good welcome and a lot of kindness shown towards us. So wait till we have some place and then do an Anthony Eden as quick as you can. He arrived on the MV *Rangitata*, I think, at Auckland day before yesterday. We heard him on the radio.

Will you have a photograph of yourselves taken with Tina for me? When you bring Tina with you she'll live on the island in the harbour [for a while] as it is the quarantine island.

I don't expect it will be very posh when we get married but that won't make any difference, and we could always spend the money on a movie that we didn't spend on impressing friends and relations. Don't worry about us love, we're both well and happy.

Look after yourselves.

God Bless

Love Jim and Rosies

In 1963, after six years in New Zealand, Rosemary visited England for almost 12 months. On her return, Rosemary and Jim received a letter from Rosemary's parents: "They said that they had booked on the *Rangitoto*, the ship I had just got off [from Rosemary's visit to England], but Mum was impatient to arrive here for the next Christmas, so they switched to the *Maasdam*. I think Mum waited to suss me out during my time in England as to whether we were happy and settled in NZ before they made up their minds to come."

In a letter to Rosemary on the voyage out, her mother wrote, "We were fools not to have the trip years ago. Whether we stay or come back I can assure you we shall have no regrets."

Rosemary's parents did stay in New Zealand.

In later years Rosemary summed up her early weeks slightly differently. In 2008 she recalled:

The correspondence was through the eyes of young folk and young folk are not hot on tolerance for things that hurt their feelings. In my case there were omissions, and I didn't mention the less pleasant things that happened. I should have, but no one wants to hear about them, and I didn't want to risk mutterings about "making one's bed and lying on it" At this distance in time we look back and laugh, but some things didn't seem so funny at the time.

We arrived on a Sunday and as New Zealand shut down at the weekends we sailed around and around the anchor chain until Monday when miraculously New Zealand came to life. We spied through binoculars at the cars driving along Oriental Parade and thought there must be a vintage car rally – we realised later that New Zealand cars were, of necessity, vintage.

We were received kindly and people were very friendly. We were "processed" on the ship and then taken out to Trentham to the Immigration Hostel. I remember a hoarding on the side of the Hutt road saying "Keep New Zealand Green", and someone had written underneath "Tell the buggers nothing". The Hostel was something else altogether.

Kiwi girls were convinced we had only come to pinch their fellas, not figuring that we brought a lot of guys, many of whom were "pinched" by Kiwi girls. I guess the anti feeling was a lot to do with so many of us being dumped on their doorstep in a comparatively short period of time, a bit like the anti Asian feeling now. I remember three of us Pom girls walking down Lambton Quay and seeing three very well-dressed, good-looking guys walking towards us all licking ice cream cornets and we all just burst out laughing. They could have been in no doubt that we were laughing at them – we wouldn't have been caught dead with a cone, only little kids had them in those days. Bet they thought we were three bitches.

One good memory was of my butcher who was Irish and a new arrival. He always gave me fillet steak and charged me gravy beef price. I wasn't sure whether he fancied me or he thought I looked hungry.

We were initially billeted at Trentham Camp, me in one part and Jim in the Post Office part. The food was deplorable by any standard, I particularly remember the unappetising tower of slowly descending, sweating toast and bilious-looking curried sausages that greeted me for breakfast, together with the guy behind the counter who possessed filthy nails and hands. There was no money left when we had paid our digs and transport into Wellington to work, not even enough to get fish and chips from the Greasy Greek.

I bought a pre-historic electric frying pan from the then Lamphouse Bargain Basement in Cuba Street. It only had two settings, "off" and "blast furnace" so my roommate Barbara and I used to seal the doors to our room, shove a bobby pin across the fuse in the hallway and cook bacon, eggs etc, anything to fill the void. Someone must have snitched that we were feeding MALES too (Oh my God!) as we were told that we would get thrown out if we didn't mend our ways. After

Jim said he couldn't eat the sandwiches the hostel provided (silverbeet sandwiches wrapped in newspaper) I would buy cheese, so we had cheese and yet more cheese. One of Jim's workmates found a note from his wife in his lunch box: "If Jim has got cheese again give him a banana". We stuck it out for about six weeks until we found a bedsit in Oriental Parade, a huge room with a world class view, and a shared kitchen to cook "real food". We left Trentham without a backward glance. We got married at St Johns Church, Trentham, a very small gathering, without any family bickering at all. Ideal! 270 Oriental Parade is now a very prodigious apartment high-rise. Gone is the wonderful kauri-built, hundred-plus-year-old house with its high ceilings and beautiful leaded lights.

It didn't really matter what your trade was, they put you where there was a need, and I did anything that paid well. Early days saw me underpaid, but there was a wonderful man at the Labour Department who championed our cause and went for the short payer and I got what was owing. I learned to stick up for myself in rather a hurry as the Kiwis short-changed us pay-wise at every opportunity, I know how the Asians feel, although we at least had language in common. I had one disadvantage: I didn't look my age and they thought I was a college kid working in the holidays.

At one shop in Lambton Quay there were three of us new Poms and we seemed to be the only ones who could do the dogsbody jobs, so when we had a combined revolt, one girl walked out and across the road to Hannahs, got a job ... to start at award wages ... and surprise, surprise, they were in excess of what we were getting. God! We must have been green and cabbage-looking. We were not supposed to change jobs whilst we were serving out our two years to pay back, in my case 89 pounds 10 shillings, but most did change. We went for the most money as that was what we needed to get ahead. The Poms and Dutch were accused of being "hungry" because we worked all hours God sent. In those days you could have had three jobs if you could have stayed awake 24 hours.

In the end I had a respectable job with the Air Department which lasted until I had done two and half years in New Zealand, we had our first house built, albeit with a mortgage, and I left to have my first baby. In fact it was 14 months after landing with £200 between us, that we moved into a brand new house. It was small, but as we had so very little in the way of furniture, that didn't matter. We have never made the rich list but we are what is known as 'comfortable'.

Food in New Zealand was good but not a great variety – but in the 50s things were not all that flash in England, either. I remember trying to buy olive oil as my Mum cooked with it. I couldn't find it, and when I asked about it, I was told to go to the chemist. Strange? I did as I was told, only to be presented with a very small bottle of it. Surely he thought I was daft when I told him I couldn't fry my chips in that drop! How far we have come in the culinary stakes.

I loved the Chinese fruit and veggie shops. New Zealand sweets were a bit strange, but you could get the English ones so that didn't matter too much. When we three Poms were working in a shoe shop, Friday night late shopping, Jim called in with a treat for us ... a Mars bar. It was awful, it was an Aussie one, yuk! Now I send Whittakers chocolate to our son in London. But I **still** miss English markets a bit. I thought the Kiwi girls very clever all making their own dresses. My mother was a dressmaker so if I got in a tangle with my efforts she always rescued me. In the early days I made a dressing gown for my new husband, boy, did I make a production of that. Shoes were awful though – solid like cardboard. My Mum knitted like a fiend for our first baby and used to send me heaps of wool from the local mill. I sent *NZ Woman's Weekly* and they sent me the English women's magazines.

We didn't have a lot of leisure time but we used to go down to the boat shed in Wellington which was used by the immigrants as a dance-cum-get-together place. We also went shooting rabbits with friends over to the Wairarapa. We would then camp and have heaps of rabbit stew. We hitch-hiked up to Rotorua the first Easter as I was dying to see boiling mud. No one had told us about the smell. There was always the pictures. It used to amuse us the way Kiwis got all dolled up, hats, gloves and all, just for the movies. Booze, then as now, seemed to be the main prop, and the six o'clock swill (no women allowed) appalled me. It seemed so uncivilised. No one seemed to have wine with a meal.

Over the years, between us we made six trips back to England. Yes, six times: first time in 1963, just me and my four-year-old son, by ship (*Rangitoto*) to see my Mum and Dad; second time in 1979 for three months (Jim's long service leave), with our two younger children; in 1985 on my own after my Dad had died; in 1991 with Jim for his Mum's 90th birthday; 2002 for our son Mike's wedding (he has lived in London for about 16 or 17 years); and in 2005 with Jim for an RAF Hornet squadron (Malaya) Reunion.

Here [New Zealand] has become "home" after 51 years and it has turned out pretty OK. Jim worked for P&T (which later changed its name to the Post Office then became Telecom) for 14 years in Wellington and Wainuiomata, then 25 years in Auckland and the rest in the beautiful Queen Charlotte Sounds.

Getting old is a bit of a bummer but it would be the same anywhere. Now comes the hard part. We had three children. Our darling Chris died 11 years ago from a brain tumour. He was 35 and left a lovely wife, Jodie, and two little boys, two and four. They are now smashing teenagers. They live in Auckland, as does Helen our daughter. Jodie is re-married to a nice guy who is making a splendid job of looking after her and the boys. We are still very close in hearts if not in distance. Helen and Steve have two children, Phoebe, four and Dylan, two. Mike in London has no children. We are close – email and phones are our lifeline.

Illustrations acknowledgement

Except where otherwise acknowledged, all photographs and other original material were supplied by Jim and Rosemary Burton (nee Thompson).

CHAPTER 18

Margaret Davies

Name	Margaret Davies
Ship	SS *Southern Cross*
Departure date	24 May 1965
Arrival date	13 July 1965
Destination	Unknown until arrival – "a farm"
Marital status	Single
Profession	Herd tester
Intention	To return after two years

I had always wanted to come to New Zealand since I was a child. I had seen a map on the wall at school and it looked okay. Although I came from a close family and was sad to be leaving them behind, I was a very independent person. Anyway, I only planned to stay the two years of the assisted passage bond and then go back to the UK. Then I would decide where I wanted to live. As it turned out, somehow I became integrated into the way of life in New Zealand and never seemed to save enough money up to return to the UK.

I didn't know much about New Zealand before I came here, and what I did know was mostly about the North Island. The South Island was just there! As it turned out, most of this information, which came from New Zealand House, turned out to not be very accurate.

There was little paperwork involved, just an entry certificate, birth certificate and an application form filled out at New Zealand House, plus an interview.

May 1965 I sailed on the SS *Southern Cross*, leaving from Southampton. I think there were about 1000-1200 mainly paying passengers, who were on a cruise. There were only 26 emigrants or "£10 Poms", as we were called – although the year I came, 1965, it cost me £25, not £10! We were in the below-waterline cabins with four in a cabin that was really tiny (couldn't swing a cat in it!), two bunks up and two down. We all had our suitcases and had to have a tin trunk too!

Very few activities were put on for us; crossing the equator ceremony, odd evening dances, and deck games. Or you could just lie in the sun and call up a waiter and have a drink! It was cheaper to drink spirits on the ship than soft drinks! I guess we were young and unattached in those days and we made our own fun. These organised activities were nothing like the on-board entertainment provided on

Margaret (at the front, in shorts) and her friend Pat. Curacao. June 1965.

today's cruises. But to me it was luxurious – waiters to serve you, lying in the sun or having a game of ball on deck, and making friends with other migrants. We did not mix with the "other" passengers, the fare-paying ones – we were definitely the lower classes! We were told to keep to our deck.

Our daily routine on board was: get up, walk around the deck, meet other migrants, talk, eat, have plenty of drinks and play a few deck games. I did get a bit bored at times, but overall it was an experience that I was glad to have had. I thoroughly enjoyed my cruise. It was exciting to be going somewhere that I knew so little about and I really enjoyed the ports of call.

On the trip I developed an eye problem. I was diagnosed as having conjunctivitis and was given penicillin injections and eye drops. A steward woke me every two hours during the night to put the drops in. But when my eye did not improve, I was sent to an eye specialist in Fiji who found that I had an eye ulcer. I could not complain about the health care on board.

We were able to leave the ship at all the ports of call, Balboa, Panama, Trinidad, Barbados, Tahiti and Fiji, sometimes for only 12 hours, sometimes up to 24 hours. We mainly ate on board the ship when we were in ports. The fun times we had at the ports were amazing. I particularly remember Trinidad, where it was safe to walk the streets, and the night clubs – well! The rum was cheaper than the coke. With rum being $1 for a large bottle and coke $10 for a bottle, guess what we drank! The people on the islands were very friendly and chatted to us, and they were happy for us to buy their wares. Panama, however, was quite dangerous, so we were encouraged not to walk around but to take taxis. Balboa was much the same. In Panama we were warned not to put our arms out of the taxi windows, as we would probably lose a hand when they snatched our watches!

I admit to feeling a bit intrepid as well as excited when we approached New Zealand. At that stage, as a herd tester, I didn't have a clue where I was going. When we docked at Wellington they put up little tables and chairs in one of the lounges and the immigration officer came on board. We were each called over and given a large buff envelope containing all the details of our contract. We had to work in the same job for two years or had to pay the New Zealand government back for our fare if we left New Zealand before our two years was up. (I never had enough money to save up the fare to go home, let alone pay them back, so I had to stay!) The envelope also had the details of my travel arrangements. I was to go south on the overnight ferry from Wellington to Christchurch, and someone would meet me when I docked. I sailed on the Inter-islander to Christchurch on the same evening that I arrived in Wellington. I did have a feed of fish and chips in Wellington beforehand. Much to my horror, it was shark! – I had never eaten that in my life!

It was with trepidation that I learnt I was going south! Back then, New Zealand was the North Island! But there are always bonuses; I found out later that herd testers who went north travelled between the farms by horse and cart, whereas I had a Ford Thames van! The farms in the south, of course, were much further apart, and would have been impossible to service by horse and cart!

I arrived in New Zealand with £1 in my pocket and was put in a bed and breakfast house whilst training. The £1 didn't go far for an evening meal, so I had to have an advance on my wages! After training in Christchurch I was transferred to Marlborough and covered farms from Kaikoura to Picton and the Rai Valley. The boss where I first trained was really good. The pay was not good but I didn't have much time to spend any as I worked 28 days non-stop per month! I worked on the farms where I tested the cows at a different farm each day, night milking and morning milking.

The farmers were just great and the wives always put on great smokos and meals – I certainly put on the weight! One of my first unusual encounters was at breakfast one morning when I had egg on toast with saveloys – I had never seen those before. And the farmer put tomato sauce over everything!

The day the herd tester came was a special day for the farmers – especially the unmarried ones! I worked with another girl; she went to one farm and I went to another each day. I remember she had a very amorous young farmer who kept her on her toes around the yard. At one farm I had a married farmer who used to creep up behind me, so one day when I had just weighed and sampled the milk and was turning to put the milk from the bucket into the vat for separating, I turned quickly and tipped the whole lot over him – he behaved himself after that.

I left herd testing after a year and worked on a poultry and eventually a pig farm in South Canterbury.

I found the towns and cities of New Zealand very different to the UK. Blenheim felt like a western town with its shop verandahs. Many things were expensive and hard to get. My Mum kept me in bras, and as duty on parcels was terrible, the value labels on the parcels were filled out accordingly – that is, understated. To buy things like tampons and other personal items was very expensive! The variety of clothing was not wide and the quality was not very good – stockings lasted one wear. Cars were really expensive. I bought a Morris Minor E (side valve) that would have been an antique in the UK.

But the farming practices here were far ahead of the UK. And farm and outdoor clothing was good and there was plenty of it. At one point I hurt my back but eventually found a chiropractor who fixed it. There were very few of them around then.

I missed my beef, and after the first month on the various farms I would gladly have thrown the sheep meat back at them, having come from the UK where we ate mainly beef and not much sheep meat. However, now I would throw the beef back! I missed decent fish and chips too. (New Zealand's are better than the UK's now!) I really missed 'Penguins', a sort of chocolate biscuit similar to a Tim-Tam. I didn't have much time for leisure as most evenings I had to go to bed early to cope with the early starts. Mostly I just chatted with the farmer's family but occasionally went to the movies, or joined the locals when they got together at their local community hall for special occasions. Later I joined a badminton club. Sports here were always strong, even in those days. I found the six o'clock closing [of the pubs] very odd! Very few people had TV for entertainment, but there were hundreds of possums! I would go out with one of the farmers the night I was there, and using a .22 we would spotlight the possums sitting on the fence posts! When I first arrived I noticed that most of the men wore shorts in the summer (a no-no in UK) and the children ran around with no shoes. I used to say before I had kids that if I ever got married and had children they would wear socks and shoes. Ha ha! My children went to school wearing shoes but they were always in their bags when they came home! When I visited the UK in 1984, my children were running around with no shoes in the Salisbury Cathedral grounds and when a couple passed me I heard one say, "Look at those poor children, they have NO shoes."

Until recently I was married to my English husband whom I met in 1973 in Temuka, South Canterbury, at a pig meeting that I was secretary of. I have three children, two girls and boy, and three grandchildren. All my children are now married and in New Zealand.

When I returned for a visit to the UK I knew why I had come to New Zealand. In the UK there were more people, more cars, more roads, more houses, more litter and their reserved attitude was the same – I loved my free life here. After I met my husband we started out share-milking and eventually owned our own farm in Southland and then progressed to a deer farm. If I had stayed in UK we would never have had our own farm.

I knew no-one when I came here so had to accept things the New Zealand way – so I became a New Zealander. The way of life here suited me. I didn't and don't have to make an appointment to have 'elevenses' (as they say in the UK) with my friends – just turn up and put the jug on! The children go to schools with grass playgrounds and swimming pools and go on camps. I became a New Zealand citizen and am proud to call myself a "Kiwi". I count my blessings and will always be grateful to the New Zealand government for choosing me to come at the rather formidable interview in New Zealand House in London!

Illustrations acknowledgement

All photographs and other original material were supplied by Margaret Holding (nee Davies).

Appendix 1

Additional letters written to the Sealey family prior to their departure from England

[Undated Letter written by Hilda, Box Wills, England to Grace Sealey]

[Hilda and Jack were people Janet's father met when working in Wiltshire as an aircraft fitter during the war. The Sealey family spent many holidays with them after the war. Janet's mother met up with Hilda again on a trip to England in 1976, the year Janet's father died.]

> My Dearest Grace
>
> Thanks for your welcome letter received okay. Well dear, I was very very sorry to hear you really are going to New Zealand. I was hoping it would fall through. Selfish of me perhaps but one doesn't like to lose one's friend. Couldn't you possibly come down for a week – just before you sail. Anyway dear, whether we see you again or not I wish you all the best in the world and I hope you will write me often when you get out there. It will be a big wrench having to leave your mother. What is Johnny going to do out there?
>
> Everything is about the same here. Sandra is dancing at the Albert Hall, London next month, but I guess you will be gone by then? I think it's somewhere about 22nd April. **When** I win the football pool I'll fly out to see you.
>
> What does Janet think of going away? Is it country or town where you are going? Well dear, write soon and if possible try & get down to see us before you go & now I'll say
>
> Cheerio and God bless.
>
> Fondest love to all from all.
>
> Your Loving Friend
>
> Hilda

[Undated letter written by Aunty Alice & Uncle Jack, London. To Mrs G Sealey.]

[Aunty Alice was a friend of Janet's paternal Grandmother. They had two sons who were her father's friends and Janet was often taken to visit them. Janet remembers them as "very special hospitable people."]

> Dear John, Grace and Janet,
>
> I thought I would like to write a few lines for the last time, in this old England of ours. The time is getting very near now & I know you must all be very excited, at the same time a big step. I hope your mum is taking it fairly well. Well it is a long way to go, but I do hope you will see in a very short time that it is all been worth it.

Dear Grace I felt I had to write just to say goodbye and wish you all everything that is good in this world, mostly.

Good health, good luck, & God bless you. I wish you all a safe and very enjoyable voyage. Don't be seasick – don't mention kippers or else!

I will close with all our fondest love to you all

From Aunt Alice & Uncle Jack

Illustrations acknowledgement

Letters were supplied by Janet Haines (nee Sealey).

Appendix 2

Documentation

The following wording is taken from the documents and correspondence retained by Janet Sealey. These documents cover part of the immigration process from the application for assisted immigrant status to the Sealey family's arrival in New Zealand.

The wording of the documents has been reproduced here, because they would have been illegible if reproduced in their original form. The majority of the documents were on large pages and in some cases in small fonts.

[Form letter L.5, undated, from the Chief Migration Officer, New Zealand Government Offices, Migration Branch, Carlton Hotel, Pall Mall, London. S.W.1. Bold below shows the fields filled in on the form.]

[The letter starts] NOTE ON GUARANTEED EMPLOYMENT. Please note that New Zealand guarantees employment and accommodation to all applicants who are accepted under the Immigration Scheme.

Dear Sir,

NOMINATIONS – New Zealand Government Immigration Scheme

I have been advised from New Zealand that you have been nominated for employment as a **Sheet metal worker by George James Hodgkinson** who has arranged accommodation for you in New Zealand at **157 Mokoia Road Birkenhead, Auckland.**

No doubt you will wish to avail yourself of this nomination and, if so, you should complete the enclosed Form (Imm.1) and return it to this Office at an early date. If, from the information supplied on your application form, you should appear to be eligible, you will be advised of the references etc. which will have to be submitted in support of your application. Should your references satisfy the Selection Committee you and, if you are married, your family, will have to be interviewed and medically examined, and, therefore, no guarantee that your application will prove successful can be given to you at this stage.

If you have previously submitted an application form for inclusion in the Scheme please let me know, at the same time advising me of your correct name and initials and address if these are not correctly shown on the envelope containing this letter. If your application is finally approved you will be given reasonable notice to enable you to dispose of your property, and you are strongly advised not to take steps to dispose of any furniture or property, or to relinquish your employment until you have been advised by this Office that arrangements have been made for you to sail on a specific vessel.

I have in conclusion to advise you that your application will be dealt with as speedily as possible, but you will appreciate that the number of applications being dealt with is very large. For this reason it will not be possible to answer telephone enquiries concerning the progress of individual applications but I shall be pleased to answer any written communications relating to your case.

Encl.Imm.1.

IMPORTANT

IT IS ESSENTIAL THAT IN ANY FUTURE CORRESPONDENCE WITH THIS OFFICE YOU SHOULD QUOTE THE REFENCE NUMBER SHOWN IN THE PANEL AT THE HEAD OF THIS LETTER AND PRINT YOUR NAME BENEATH YOUR SIGNATURE.

Mr J.H. Sealey.

[Document entitled 'Immigration Scheme'. Original document 34 x 21 cm, typed on both sides.]

PART 1.

GENERAL CONDITIONS.

The New Zealand Government will accept eligible persons, subject to the limitations indicated below, provided that they are medically fit and are otherwise regarded as suitable for settlement in New Zealand. The decision whether an individual can or cannot be accepted as a settler rests with the New Zealand Government, which arranges through the New Zealand High Commissioner in London, for the selection and medical examination of applicants.

For the time being the Scheme is limited to persons required for employment in certain occupations.

Married persons cannot be accepted if there is an estrangement and they are separated and living apart. Widows, widowers or divorced persons with dependent children cannot be considered unless they are nominated by friends, relatives or prospective employers in New Zealand who are able to guarantee adequate accommodation for all the members of the family and they are prepared to accept employment in a productive or servicing industry. Relatives, friends or employers in New Zealand must have nominations approved by the Department of Labour and Employment in New Zealand. The Department does not arrange nominations or contacts between people in the United Kingdom and prospective nominators in New Zealand.

The trades and occupations for which applicants are being accepted and the age groups, may be ascertained from the Chief Migration Officer, New Zealand Migration Offices, Carlton Hotel Building, Pall Mall, London, S.W.1., and at all Local Offices of the Ministry of Labour.

Applications for free passages are limited to persons of British nationality and of European race and colour who have resided permanently in the United Kingdom. Persons who served overseas with the United Kingdom Armed Forces of Merchant Navy are deemed to have been ordinarily resident in the United Kingdom during the period of such service. (There is also provision for assisted passages for nationals of certain North and West European countries who are single, of European race and colour and have resided in the United Kingdom for 12 months. Details are obtainable from the New Zealand Migration Offices in London).

The maximum age limit is 45 years, but in some cases a lower age limit applies.

NEW ZEALAND.

IN YOUR REPLY PLEASE REFER TO

IMM.142786

L.5

TELEGRAPHIC ADDRESS:
"DEPUTY, LONDON"

TELEPHONE:
TRAFALGAR
7040

NEW ZEALAND GOVERNMENT OFFICES,
MIGRATION BRANCH,
CARLTON HOTEL,
PALL MALL,
LONDON, S.W.1.

> **NOTE ON GUARANTEED EMPLOYMENT**
> Please note that New Zealand guarantees employment
> and accommodation to all applicants who are accepted
> under the Immigration Scheme.

Dear Sir/~~Madam~~

NOMINATIONS
New Zealand Government Immigration Scheme

I have been advised from New Zealand that you have been nominated for employment as a **Sheet metal worker** by **George James Hodgkinson** who has arranged accommodation for you in New Zealand at **157 Mokoia Road Birkenhead, Auckland.**

No doubt you will wish to avail yourself of this nomination and, if so, you should complete the enclosed Form (Imm.1) and return it to this Office at an early date. If, from the information supplied on your application form, you appear to be eligible, you will be advised of the references etc. which will have to be submitted in support of your application. Should your references satisfy the Selection Committee you and, if you are married, your family, will have to be interviewed and medically examined, and, therefore, no guarantee that your application will prove successful can be given to you at this stage.

If you have previously submitted an application form for inclusion in the Scheme please let me know, at the same time advising me of your correct name and initials and address if these are not correctly shown on the envelope containing this letter.

If your application is finally approved you will be given reasonable notice to enable you to dispose of your property, and you are strongly advised not to take steps to dispose of any furniture or property, or to relinquish your employment until you have been advised by this Office that arrangements have been made for you to sail on a specific vessel.

I have in conclusion to advise you that your application will be dealt with as speedily as possible, but you will appreciate that the number of applications being dealt with is very large. For this reason it will not be possible to answer telephone enquiries concerning the progress of individual applications but I shall be pleased to answer any written communications relating to your case.

Yours faithfully,

Smith

Chief Migration Officer

Encl.Imm.1.

IMPORTANT

IT IS ESSENTIAL THAT IN ANY FUTURE CORRESPONDENCE WITH THIS OFFICE YOU SHOULD QUOTE THE REFERENCE NUMBER SHOWN IN THE PANEL AT THE HEAD OF THIS LETTER AND PRINT YOUR NAME BENEATH YOUR SIGNATURE.

Mr J.H. Sealey.

Form letter L.5 advising John Sealey of his having been nominated for employment in New Zealand.

PART 2.

WHAT IS REQUIRED OF APPLICANTS.

Applicants have to qualify in accordance with the conditions set out in Part 1 above. They also have to pass medical and X-Ray examinations to be arranged and paid for by the New Zealand Government and to complete contracts with the New Zealand Government which include the terms set out in Part 3 below. Applicants who are selected are not required to obtain passports, as Documents of Identity are issued free by the Chief Migration Officer.

It will be noticed that in Clause (1) of Part 3 below, the applicant undertakes to accept and to remain for two years in the employment to which he is allocated by the Director of Employment. The Director, in the exercise of his authority, pays due regard to the locality preference expressed by the applicant, the needs of particular localities, and the precise nature of the work carried out by individual employers in relation to the National requirements. Applicants who are not nominated have to be prepared to accept employment anywhere in New Zealand, as it is not always possible to place them in the particular locality for which a preference is expressed. (The Director of Employment is the Permanent Head of the Department of Labour and Employment in New Zealand).

PART 3.

DETAILS OF THE AGREEMENT TO BE COMPLETED LATER BY SUCCESSFUL APPLICANTS.

Successful applicants are required to execute a form of agreement with the New Zealand Government which includes the following clauses:-

1. THAT I will immediately upon my arrival in New Zealand engage in employment as a .... (occupation) and will remain in the employment to which I am allocated by the Director of Employment, at the rates currently payable, for a continuous period of two years.

2. THAT in the event of my failing to comply fully with any of the terms of this agreement, but not otherwise, I will refund to the New Zealand Government the sum paid in respect of steamship passage(s) for myself (and my family).

NOTE:

The sum of money to be expressed in Clause (2) will be the amount advanced to the applicant for the steamship fare(s) from port of embarkation in the United Kingdom to port of disembarkation in New Zealand, i.e., the full fare, which usually ranges from £75 to £125 sterling for adults.

INFORMATION FOR APPLICANTS.

READ CAREFULLY.

Applicants are warned against leaving their employment, vacating their residences, or disposing of their property until advised in writing by the Chief Migration Officer of a definite sailing date.

INTERVIEWING CENTRES.

See Question (2) (b) on the front page of the application form and in your answer to it name the centre at which it would be most convenient for you to have your interview. The interviewing centres are shown below:

Aberdeen	Dumfries	Luton	Preston
Ayr	Edinburgh	Lerwick	Portadown
Barnstable	Elgin	London	Scarborough
Barrow	Enniskillen	Londonderry	Sheffield
Birmingham	Exeter	Llandrindod Wells	Shrewsbury
Boston	Glasgow	Manchester	Southampton
Bristol	Guernsey	Marlborough	Stafford
Belfast	Hastings	Middlesbrough	Swansea
Ballymena	Hereford	Newcastle	Stornaway
Cambridge	Hull	Norwich	Taunton
Cardiff	Inverness	Nottingham	Thurso
Cardigan	Ipswich	Oban	Truro
Carlisle	Jersey	Omagh	Worcester
Colwyn Bay	Kettering	Oxford	Wrexham
Coventry	King's Lynn	Perth	Yeovil
Doncaster	Leeds	Peterborough	York
Dorchester	Leicester	Pitlochry	
Dover	Lincoln	Portmadoc	
Dundee	Liverpool	Plymouth	

If selected for interview you will be asked by letter to submit:

(a)   Birth Certificates.

(b)   Marriage Certificate.

(c)   If widowed, death certificate of wife or husband.

(d)   If a tradesman, proof of your trade qualifications and experience in the form of evidence from a previous employer, together with apprenticeship certificate or indenture.

(e)   If ex-service, your service discharge papers.

IMMIGRATION SCHEME.

PART 1.

GENERAL CONDITIONS.

The New Zealand Government will accept eligible persons, subject to the limitations indicated below, provided that they are medically fit and are otherwise regarded as suitable for settlement in New Zealand. The decision whether an individual can or cannot be accepted as a settler rests with the New Zealand Government, which arranges through the New Zealand High Commissioner in London, for the selection and medical examination of applicants.

For the time being the Scheme is limited to persons required for employment in certain occupations.

Married persons cannot be accepted if there is an estrangement and they are separated and living apart. Widows, widowers or divorced persons with dependent children cannot be considered unless they are nominated by friends, relatives or prospective employers in New Zealand who are able to guarantee adequate accommodation for all the members of the family and they are prepared to accept employment in a productive or servicing industry. Relatives, friends or employers in New Zealand must have nominations approved by the Department of Labour and Employment in New Zealand. The Department does not arrange nominations or contacts between people in the United Kingdom and prospective nominators in New Zealand.

The trades and occupations for which applicants are being accepted and the age groups, may be ascertained from the Chief Migration Officer, New Zealand Migration Offices, Carlton Hotel Building, Pall Mall, London, S.W.1., and at all Local Offices of the Ministry of Labour.

Applications for free passages are limited to persons of British nationality and of European race and colour who have resided permanently in the United Kingdom. Persons who served overseas with the United Kingdom Armed Forces or Merchant Navy are deemed to have been ordinarily resident in the United Kingdom during the period of such service. (There is also provision for assisted passages for nationals of certain North and West European countries who are single, of European race and colour and have resided in the United Kingdom for 12 months. Details are obtainable from the New Zealand Migration Offices in London).

The maximum age limit is 45 years, but in some cases a lower age limit applies.

PART 2.

WHAT IS REQUIRED OF APPLICANTS.

Applicants have to qualify in accordance with the conditions set out in Part 1 above. They also have to pass medical and X-Ray examinations to be arranged and paid for by the New Zealand Government and to complete contracts with the New Zealand Government which include the terms set out in Part 3 below. Applicants who are selected are not required to obtain passports, as Documents of Identity are issued free by the Chief Migration Officer.

It will be noticed that in Clause (1) of Part 3 below, the applicant undertakes to accept and to remain for two years in the employment to which he is allocated by the Director of Employment. The Director, in the exercise of his authority, pays due regard to the locality preference expressed by the applicant, the needs of particular localities, and the precise nature of the work carried out by individual employers in relation to the National requirements. Applicants who are not nominated have to be prepared to accept employment anywhere in New Zealand, as it is not always possible to place them in the particular locality for which a preference is expressed. (The Director of Employment is the Permanent Head of the Department of Labour and Employment in New Zealand).

PLEASE DETACH AND RETAIN THIS SHEET.

First page of the document – Immigration Scheme.

[Single page entitled 'Prospects of Settlement – Amendments'. From the Chief Migration Offices. January 1953.]

Foreword and Page 5. The limited amount of accommodation being provided by the Government for married tradesmen has been fully taken up. The only married persons now eligible are skilled workers who can obtain nominations and who have not more than two dependent children.

Page 8: PASSAGES. The usual waiting period before embarkation is between six and nine months from the date of application.

Page 10: PASSING THE CUSTOMS. There is now no limit to the value of "household or other effects" and "implements, instruments, tools of trade, occupation or profession" which may be taken into New Zealand, provided they have been in use by the passenger for not less than twelve months prior to embarkation.

It is the practice to allow bicycles, motor-cycles and motor-cars to be included within the term "household or other effects, "provided they have been in use by the persons or families bringing them to New Zealand for not less than twelve months prior to embarkation."

Page 12: WAGE RATES. All minimum Award rates of wages have been increased by 10s. to 14s. per week. Award wages now range from £8 11s. 3d. a week for labourers to over £10 9s. 0d. for some skilled tradesmen. Minimum rates for women range from £6 6s. 10d. for skilled clothing workers and £5 18s. 1d. for hospital ward maids.

Page 14: CURRENT PRICES.

Butter	1s 8d lb
Meat from	1s 0d to 2s 6d lb
Bread	6.1/2d a 2lb loaf.

Pages 16 and 17: INCOME TAX. The surcharge has been reduced to 5 per cent. and the rebate increased to £15. The following is an example of income tax paid by a married man with two dependent children on an income of £600 a year and assuming a £20 exemption for life insurance premiums:

	£	s	d	£	s	d
Assessable income is				600	0	0
Deduct exemptions:						
Personal	200	0	0			
Wife	100	0	0			
Children (two)	100	0	0			
Life Insurance premiums	20	0	0			
				420	0	0
Taxable balance is				180	0	0
Income tax at 2s. 6d. in £ on £100	12	10	0			
Income tax at 2s. 9d. in £ on £80	11	0	0			
				23	10	0
Plus 5 per cent.				1	3	6
				24	13	6
Less special rebate				15	0	0
Income tax payable				£9	13	6

On an income of £600, such a person would pay £45 Social Security tax over the period, but would have received back £52 as family benefit (10s. per week for each child) as well as other benefits.

For a single person on an income of £600 a year, and assuming an exemption of £20 for life insurance premiums, income tax (excluding Social Security) would amount to £41 19s. 3d.

The double taxation agreement referred to on page 17 is an agreement designed to relieve taxpayers from the payment of tax in both countries on the same income.

[Form letter L.52(M), dated 24 September 1953, from the Chief Migration Officer, New Zealand Government Offices, Migration Branch, Carlton Hotel, Pall Mall, London. S.W.1.]

Dear Sir,

New Zealand Immigration Scheme

I am pleased to be able to tell you that your application is progressing well and that an interview with one of my representatives will be arranged for you as soon as possible. You will be advised later of the time and place of the interview, at which your wife and children (if any) will also have to attend.

I should like to remind you that when you attend for interview it will be necessary for you to take with you any of the following documents that you have not already produced and that are applicable to you:-

Marriage Certificate

Birth Certificates for yourself and each member of your family

Service Discharge Papers

A recent school report on each child attending school.

The attached leaflet covering employment and living conditions is self-explanatory. Please sign one copy of this and hand it to my representative at the time of interview. The other copy is for you to keep. At the time of your interview you will be given every opportunity of discussing the contents of the leaflet if you so desire.

It may be that you have friends who have also applied under the Immigration Scheme. If so, they may or may not be interviewed about the same time as yourselves, depending on how far their application has progressed. If they are not called for interview when you are, this does not necessarily mean that their application is not going to be successful.

You would be well advised to keep this letter as a reminder of the documents you will need to take with you to your interview.

Encl: L.44

[The following is typed at the bottom of the form letter] P.S. Please reply to paragraph 5 of my letter L.13M.

IN YOUR REPLY PLEASE REFER TO

Imm. 142786

NEW ZEALAND.

L.52(M)

NEW ZEALAND GOVERNMENT OFFICES,

MIGRATION BRANCH,

CARLTON HOTEL,

PALL MALL,

LONDON, S.W.1.

24 September 1953.

TELEGRAPHIC ADDRESS:
"DEPUTY, LONDON"

TELEPHONE:
TRAFALGAR
7040

NOTE ON GUARANTEED EMPLOYMENT

Please note that New Zealand guarantees employment and accommodation to all applicants who are accepted under the Immigration Scheme.

Dear Sir,

New Zealand Immigration Scheme

I am pleased to be able to tell you that your application is progressing well and that an interview with one of my representatives will be arranged for you as soon as possible. You will be advised later of the time and place of the interview, at which your wife and children (if any) will also have to attend.

I should like to remind you that when you attend for interview it will be necessary for you to take with you <u>any of the following documents that you have not already produced and that are applicable to you</u>:-

      Marriage Certificate
      Birth Certificates for yourself and each member of your family
      Service Discharge Papers
      A recent school report on each child attending school.

The attached leaflet covering employment and living conditions is self-explanatory. Please sign one copy of this and hand it to my representative at the time of interview. The other copy is for you to keep. At the time of your interview you will be given every opportunity of discussing the contents of the leaflet if you so desire.

It may be that you have friends who have also applied under the Immigration Scheme. If so, they may or may not be interviewed about the same time as yourselves, depending on how far their application has progressed. If they are not called for interview when you are, this does not necessarily mean that their application is not going to be successful.

You would be well advised to keep this letter as a reminder of the documents you will need to take with you to your interview.

Yours faithfully,

Chief Migration Officer.

Encl: L.44

IMPORTANT

IT IS ESSENTIAL THAT IN ANY FUTURE CORRESPONDENCE WITH THIS OFFICE YOU SHOULD QUOTE THE REFERENCE NUMBER SHOWN IN THE PANEL AT THE HEAD OF THIS LETTER AND PRINT YOUR NAME BENEATH YOUR SIGNATURE.

P.S. Please reply to paragraph 5 of my letter L.15M.

Form letter L.52 (M) advising John Sealey of the progress of his application for immigration to New Zealand.

[Letter dated 24 November 1953, from the Chief Migration Officer, New Zealand Government Offices, Migration Branch, Carlton Hotel, Pall Mall, London. S.W.1. To Mr J.H. Sealey, Flat 2, 49 Champion Hill, London S.E.5.]

Dear Mr Sealey,

I am pleased to tell you that employment is available to you as a Sheet Metal Erector at Modern Sheet Metal Limited, Auckland, at 5/4½d per hour to commence.

Please note that the employment conditions outlined above are those which apply at the present time and are subject to variation according to circumstances beyond the control of the Immigration Authorities in New Zealand.

I assume that you are prepared to accept this employment, and I am enclosing an amended agreement form which you should sign in the presence of a responsible witness and return to me as soon as possible. Please note that the agreement form should be signed and dated on the front only; the part on the back of the form is not to be completed until you arrive in New Zealand. Also please note that your signature must be witnessed by a Justice of the Peace, Clergyman, Postmaster, Bank Manager or Police Officer.

I should also like you to have your medical and x-ray examinations, and for this purpose I enclose letters addressed to Dr Marr and Dr Rackow with whom you should arrange appointments and hand the enclosures to the respective doctors at the time that you attend.

[Form letter Imm.9, dated 15 January 1954, signed for from the Chief Migration Officer, New Zealand Government Offices, Migration Branch, Carlton Hotel, Pall Mall, London. S.W.1. Bold below shows the fields filled in on the form.]

I am pleased to be able to tell you that your application for free passage(s) to New Zealand has been accepted and your case has been referred to the Shipping Section of this Office.

Arrangements will be made for you to sail during **April/May 1954** or possibly earlier should suitable accommodation become available on a ship leaving before this time. In making your preparations you can assume that you will sail not later than **May 1954** but I cannot guarantee that you will sail before that month.

In the normal course of events, sailing instructions will be issued to you approximately two months before the date of embarkation and these will give you full details of all passage arrangements. The notice of sailing you will require may have some bearing on whether I can arrange for you to sail earlier than the time indicated above. If you wish to be considered for any earlier sailing, will you please let me know what is the absolute minimum notice of sailing that you could accept.

[Letter dated 1 February 1954, signed for from the Chief Migration Officer, New Zealand Government Offices, Migration Branch, Carlton Hotel, Pall Mall, London. S.W.1. To Mr J.H. Sealey, Flat 2, 49 Champion Hill, London S.E.5.]

I acknowledge receipt of your letter of the 27 January, but must advise you that I have been asked by your proposed employer in New Zealand to expedite your embarkation. In the circumstances I must ask whether you could not make arrangements to be available for sailing on the T.S.S. "Captain Cook" on the 13 April.

[Letter dated 10 February 1954, signed for from the Chief Migration Officer, New Zealand Government Offices, Migration Branch, Carlton Hotel, Pall Mall, London. S.W.1. To Mr J.H. Sealey, Flat 2, 49 Champion Hill, London S.E.5.]

I wish to acknowledge receipt on 5 February of your wife's recent letter, from which I see that you are prepared to sail in April, although you would prefer the sailing to be deferred.

As I explained to you in my previous letter, your future employer has asked that your embarkation be expedited and if I do not arrange for your embarkation in April, there is always the possibility that he may not be prepared to hold the job open.

In these circumstances, I strongly recommend that you accept the embarkation date I have offered of 13 April. As it seems you reluctantly accepted this date in your last letter, I would like you to confirm by return of post that 13 April would be a suitable embarkation date for you.

[Form letter dated 2 March 1954, from J.B.Westray & Co. Limited, 138 Leadenhall Street, London E.C.3. Addressed to Dear Sir/Madam.]

T.S.S. "CAPTAIN COOK"

Referring to your passage to New Zealand in the above vessel, which is expected to sail from Glasgow on Tuesday, 13th April, 1954, we enclose baggage instructions in respect of baggage to be sent in advance to Glasgow.

Embarkation Instructions and Steamer Ticket will be forwarded as soon as the date of sailing is confirmed.

[Form letter, undated, from the Chief Migration Officer, New Zealand Government Offices, Migration Branch, Carlton Hotel, Pall Mall, London. S.W.1.]

DRAFT No.35. T.S.S. "Captain Cook". Sailing from Glasgow about 13 April 1954

Passages to New Zealand have been arranged for you and you wife (and child/ren) on the above-named vessel. If you will be available for sailing, please complete the attached Board of Trade form and return it to the Shipping Company named. You will then receive your steamship ticket in due course, together with further details concerning the exact date, time and place of embarkation.

A Railway Warrant for the journey to Glasgow is attached and will be changed for a ticket only at the station named. A Document of Identity, which serves in lieu of a passport is enclosed unless you have already notified this Office that you have a valid passport. This document should be checked by you and if any detail is incorrect or has been omitted it must be returned for re-issue. If you find it necessary to spend the night prior to embarkation away from your home you must make your own arrangements for accommodation.

The enclosed "Disposal of Baggage" form should be completed shortly before sailing and retained ready to hand in immediately prior to embarkation at Glasgow. The "Captain Cook" will proceed to New Zealand on the direct route via Curacao in the Dutch West Indies and Panama Canal. Passengers who wish to go ashore in the Panama Canal Zone will be required by the American Authorities to produce a valid Ministry of Health International Certificate of Vaccination against Smallpox. This form is attached and will need to be completed by your local doctor at your own expense. Failure to produce such a certificate may result in the passenger being refused permission to go ashore in the Panama Canal Zone. Following vaccination the arm sometimes becomes swollen and painful, and can cause considerable discomfort, and it is strongly recommended that passengers should be vaccinated at least four weeks before embarkation.

Your attention is drawn to the information contained in the attached leaflet "Notes for Passengers", which should be studied carefully. You are asked to note particularly the instructions regarding baggage. Every endeavour is made to accommodate family groups together in two or four-berth cabins, but you are reminded that this is not possible in every case and it may be necessary for your family to be separated. Expectant mothers will not be permitted to embark if the date of confinement is less than three months from the date of embarkation and it is important that this Office be informed in all such cases.

A ship's doctor and a staff of fully qualified nursing sisters are carried on the ship but parents must realize that they will be responsible for the supervision, personal hygiene and, in minor illnesses, the nursing of their own children.

Please notify any change of address to this Office and to the Shipping Company. If, for any reason, you are unable to sail, please be good enough to advise me by telegram. This will help me to allot your berth to another passenger.

Encl: Rail Warrant, Baggage Form, Vaccination Certs., Insurance Form, Board of Trade Form, Baggage Labels, Shipping Company's Leaflet, Document of Identity, Notes for Passengers.

N.º   18603

New Zealand Govt. Offices,
Migration Branch,
Carlton Hotel,
London, S.W.1.

THIS DOCUMENT IS NOT
VALID AFTER:

13 July 1954

NEW ZEALAND
DOCUMENT OF IDENTITY

Issued in lieu of a Passport for travel to New Zealand
as an approved migrant to:

Name   JOHN HENRY SEALEY

accompanied by his wife   GRACE MARGARET SEALEY

DESCRIPTION:

	BEARER	WIFE
Nationality	British	British
Place of birth	London	London
Date of birth	13.1.1911	11.7.1911
Height	5 ft. 8½ ins.	5 ft. 4 ins.
Colour of eyes	Hazel	Blue
Colour of hair	Brown	Fair
Special peculiarities	NIL	NIL

CHILDREN

Name	Date of birth	Sex
JANET MAVOURNEEN SEALEY	15.9.1940	Female

SIGNATURE OF BEARER :   *J. Sealey.*

SIGNATURE OF WIFE :   *G. Sealey.*

M.C. Smith
Chief Migration Officer.

This document is valid for a single journey only and must be surrendered to the
Immigration Authorities at the Port of Disembarkation in New Zealand.

New Zealand Document of Identity for John Sealey and family

[Two pages comprising the Notes for Passengers referred to in the previous form letter.]

NOTES FOR PASSENGERS – FAMILY GROUPS

1. EXPENSES

The average traveller to New Zealand spends between £6 and £10 during the voyage. In addition, it is very desirable to have a further £10 for expenses during the time between arrival in New Zealand and your first pay-day. It follows that you should try to embark with at least £20. Passengers are not permitted to leave the United Kingdom with more than £5 in notes and £1 in silver, but travellers' cheques may be taken and these are negotiable on the ship and in New Zealand. Travellers' cheques can be obtained from any Bank or Travel Agency.

2. BANK ACCOUNTS

Can be transferred without restriction through normal banking channels. Post Office accounts can be transferred to the New Zealand Savings Bank on application to the Savings Bank Division, Harrogate, Yorkshire.

3. SPECIAL FOODS FOR CHILDREN

National Dried Milk is not available on board ship, although other brands of dried milk, such as Cow-and Gate, Ostermilk and condensed or unsweetened, in addition to other types of baby foods, are available free of charge. Parents who prefer that their children continue on National Dried Milk, or any other special brand, are advised to apply to their local Food Office for a sufficient supply to last a five-week voyage.

4. BAGGAGE

The Shipping Company will allow each passenger to carry 20 cubic feet of personal baggage without charge. Any excess must be paid for at the rate of 6/6d per cubic foot. Children of one and two years are permitted one quarter of the adult allowance and from three to eleven years, half. Personal baggage is restricted to clothing and effects and if you intend to take any household effects such as furniture, crockery, linen, blankets, etc., you must contact the Shipping Company and they will advise whether it will be necessary to send these articles as freight. Any freight charges incurred will be your own responsibility. Children's unpacked perambulators are carried free but their use on board is at the discretion of the Commander. As a special concession tools of trade will be accepted as personal baggage.

The transport of baggage and effects from your home to the ship's side is your own responsibility. On arrival in New Zealand the Department of Labour and Employment will arrange for the collection of heavy luggage (but not items shipped as freight, or cycles and motor cycles) and for its delivery to your ultimate destination, but it will not accept liability for loss or damage (see paragraph 11). It is in your interests to insure baggage before departure. To facilitate handling in New Zealand, please note the following:-

One of the enclosed labels must be affixed to each end of each package in addition to the labels which will be supplied by the Shipping Company.

All the personal baggage of your family (but not items shipped as freight or cycles and motor cycles) must be labelled in block letters with full Christian names and Surname of the head of the family and addressed:- c/o Department of Labour and Employment, Draft No. – (this number is shown on the top right hand corner of the previous page), Wellington, New Zealand. In no circumstances should a private address be shown on PERSONAL luggage. Nominated passengers should note this instruction. It is emphasised that all luggage for your family must bear only the name of the husband or head of the family.

A supply of "stick-on" labels will shortly be forwarded to you by our shipping agents, and these labels should be affixed to all pieces of baggage. "Stick-on" labels are liable to peel off, particularly from rough surfaces, and to avoid loss in transit it is imperative that a stout tie-on label be attached to the handles of cabin trunks, suitcases, hat boxes, etc. As a further safeguard it is suggested that your name be painted or stencilled on your heavy luggage. Before embarkation, ensure that your heavy baggage is strongly secured. Tools of trade must be packed in strengthened cases and marked "Tool Box".

Baggage not required during the voyage should be labelled "not wanted on voyage". Baggage required during the voyage should be labelled "Baggage Room" and you will have access to this at frequent intervals. It is advisable to pack clothing required for the first few days at sea and toilet requisites in one suitcase labelled "Cabin".

[Continued on second page]

Any quantity of luggage in excess of 1000 lbs. per person will be subject to surcharge by the Railways in this country and in New Zealand, and the cost will have to be met by you.

5. PACKING MATERIAL

Because of the risk of the introduction of disease into New Zealand please note that use of hay, straw or chaff as packing material is prohibited. For the same reason the introduction of any soil, sand, clay or earth, whether by itself or adhering to boots, implements, or any other goods, is also prohibited.

6. DENTAL TREATMENT

Doctors are not expert dentists, and passengers requiring attention to their teeth should have them seen to before embarkation to guard against the possibility of discomfort on the voyage.

7. RATION BOOKS

Passengers are required to surrender Ration Books and National Health Service Medical Cards at the embarkation. Section "A" of page 5 of the Ration Book must be completed before arrival at the port.

8. WORKING CLOTHES

Manual workers should take suitable working clothes. These should be carried in hand baggage so that they are readily available upon disembarkation.

9. ADDRESS IN NEW ZEALAND

Until you have a permanent address in New Zealand, letters may be addressed to you – c/o Immigration Division, Department of Labour and Employment, Draft No. – (as shown in top right-hand corner on previous page), Wellington, New Zealand.

10. FARES

Your fares to New Zealand will cost between £82 and £130 each, depending upon the shipping accommodation allotted to you. The cost will be recoverable only in the event of your failure to comply with the terms of the Agreement and Undertaking into which you have entered with the New Zealand Government.

11. HANDLING OF BAGGAGE IN NEW ZEALAND

When you arrive at Wellington you will be greeted by Officials of the Department of Labour and Employment. Part of their service to you will be in the handling of your heavy luggage from the moment it leaves the ship and right through to delivery to your final destination in New Zealand. Dealing with so many thousands of pieces of luggage is a difficult task but you can help by remembering the following rules:-

(1) Personal luggage includes blankets, linen, cutlery, crockery but not furniture, refrigerators, washing machines, bicycles or similar bulky articles.

(2) When you leave the ship remember to carry sufficient clothing etc. for your immediate requirements. It may take up to three weeks before your heavy luggage arrives at your destination.

(3) Label all personal baggage of your family in the name of the husband or head of the family.

(4) Label all personal baggage c/o Department of Labour and Employment as shown in the attached sailing instructions.

(5) Contact the Shipping Company regarding freight or merchandise such as furniture and similar bulky articles.

(6) Consign merchandise to your final destination in New Zealand and label it accordingly.

(7) Remember that merchandise will not be handled by the Department of Labour and Employment.

(8) Read carefully the notes on the attached baggage form and complete the form accordingly.

(9) Do not include merchandise (furniture, refrigerators, etc) in the "Disposal of Baggage" form.

[TSS Captain Cook Embarkation Notice to Passengers – London and Home Counties, dated 26 March 1954. From The New Zealand Shipping Company Ltd]

T.S.S. CAPTAIN COOK

EMBARKATION NOTICE TO PASSENGERS

LONDON AND HOME COUNTIES

EMBARKATION WILL TAKE PLACE AT GLASGOW, BERTH No. 65, PLANTATION QUAY, ON TUESDAY, 13th APRIL, 1954.

BOAT TRAIN.

For the convenience of passengers travelling from or *via* London, a special train consisting of Third Class coaches only, will depart from **Euston Station, London**, at **9.17 p.m.** on **Monday, 12th April** for **St. Enoch Station, Glasgow.** Passengers should provide themselves with refreshments for the night journey in the train. No sleeper accommodation is available.

Passengers (with the exception of those travelling under the New Zealand Government's Immigration Scheme who are in possession of travel warrants) pay their own fares and tickets may be obtained at the **Main Line Booking Office, Euston Station.**

Representatives of our Glasgow Agents will meet the train on arrival and passengers should ensure their baggage is loaded into road vans which will be standing by to transport all baggage, free of charge, direct to **Plantation Quay.**

BREAKFASTS.

The restaurants detailed overleaf open at the times stated and are within walking distance from the Station. Passengers will, therefore, have an opportunity of purchasing breakfast before proceeding to the Docks **from St. Enoch Railway Station, Glasgow.**

TRANSPORT FACILITIES IN GLASGOW.

Motor Coaches labelled " Captain Cook " will leave from the Carriageway, alongside **No. 6 Platform, St. Enoch Station, Glasgow,** commencing at **9.00 a.m. until 10.00 a.m.** to convey passengers, free of charge, to **Plantation Quay.**

W.V.S. will be in attendance at the Station and Dock to assist with young children, and a Canteen adjacent to the Ship's Berth will be open to passengers requiring tea, etc., which will be provided at moderate charges.

BERTHING CARDS will be handed to passengers when embarking.

DOCUMENTS.

On reaching the place of embarkation, passengers are requested to have readily available the undermentioned documents.

1. Passage Ticket and Embarkation Counterfoil.
2. Ration Book and Medical Cards.
*3. New Zealand Government Baggage Form.

*This refers to passengers travelling under the New Zealand Government Immigration Scheme.

RATION BOOKS AND MEDICAL CARDS.

Ration Books should be in the personal possession of passengers when they embark as they may be required for inspection by the Immigration Officer. Section A of page 5 of the Ration Book should be completed before arrival at the port of embarkation if the passenger intends to leave the country for more than three months, and in this event he should also bring his National Health Service Medical Card, as this should be surrendered.

EXCESS BAGGAGE CHARGES.

All charges for Excess Baggage, including Bicycles, must be paid when passengers embark. Passengers concerned should therefore provide themselves with the necessary cash for this purpose (Travellers Cheques in small denominations can also be accepted).

If time permits however, debit notes will be sent by P. Henderson & Co., to passengers' last known address, and payment of such debits should be made by return of post.

(P.T.O.)

Front Page of the TSS Captain Cook Embarkation Notice to Passengers – London and Home Counties.

EMBARKATION WILL TAKE PLACE AT GLASGOW, BERTH No. 65, PLANTATION QUAY, ON TUESDAY, 13th APRIL, 1954.

BOAT TRAIN

For the convenience of passengers travelling from or via London, a special train consisting of Third Class coaches only, will depart from Euston Station, London, at 9:17p.m. on Monday, 12th April for St. Enoch Station, Glasgow. Passengers should provide themselves with refreshments for the night journey in the train. No sleeper accommodation is available.

Passengers (with the exception of those travelling under the New Zealand Government's Immigration Scheme who are in possession of travel warrants) pay their own fares and tickets may be obtained at the Main Line Booking Office, Euston Station.

Representatives of our Glasgow Agents will meet the train on arrival and passengers should ensure their baggage is loaded into road vans which will be standing by to transport all baggage, free of charge, direct to Plantation Quay.

BREAKFASTS

The restaurants detailed overleaf open at the times stated and are within walking distance from the station. Passengers will, therefore, have an opportunity of purchasing breakfast before proceeding to the Docks from St. Enoch Railway Station, Glasgow.

TRANSPORT FACILITIES IN GLASGOW.

Motor Coaches labelled "Captain Cook" will leave from the Carriageway, alongside No. 6 Platform, St. Enoch Station, Glasgow, commencing at 9.00a.m. until 10.00a.m. to convey passengers, free of charge, to Plantation Quay.

W.V.S. will be in attendance at the Station and Dock to assist with young children, and a Canteen adjacent to the Ship's Berth will be open to passengers requiring tea, etc., which will be provided at moderate charges.

BERTHING CARDS will be handed to passengers when embarking.

DOCUMENTS

On reaching the place of embarkation, passengers are requested to have readily available the undermentioned documents.

1.   Passage Ticket and Embarkation Counterfoil.
2.   Ration Book and Medical Cards.
3.   * New Zealand Government Baggage Form.

*This refers to passengers travelling under the New Zealand Government Immigration Scheme.

RATION BOOKS AND MEDICAL CARDS

Ration Books should be in the personal possession of passengers when they embark as they may be required for inspection by the Immigration Officer. Section A of page 5 of the Ration Book should be completed before arrival at the port of embarkation if the passenger intends to leave the country for more than three months, and in this event he should also bring his National Health Service Medical Card, as this should be surrendered.

EXCESS BAGGAGE CHARGES

All charges for Excess Baggage, including Bicycles, must be paid when passengers embark. Passengers concerned should therefore provide themselves with the necessary cash for this purpose

(Travellers Cheques in small denominations can also be accepted).

If time permits however, debit notes will be sent by P. Henderson & Co. [Glasgow agents of The New Zealand Shipping Co. Ltd] to passengers' last known address, and payment of such debits should be made by return of post.

[Continued on second page]

CURRENCY

Passengers are reminded of H.M. Treasury restrictions against taking more than £5 per person in English Sterling notes and £1 in silver out of this country without a certificate. In addition the equivalent of £10 in New Zealand Currency may be carried.

Passengers are warned that when they present themselves at the port of embarkation they will be questioned by the United Kingdom Immigration Officer and any money in excess of the amount permitted, and for which they do not hold a certificate, will be detained and will be liable to confiscation.

RELATIVES AND FRIENDS

It is regretted that owing to Government Regulations visitors cannot be allowed on board, and relatives and friends should not therefore travel to Glasgow.

NOTE

It is essential that Passengers keep us advised as to any change of address.

WARNING

In view of the acute shortage of passenger accommodation which still persists, it is important that no ship should sail with vacant berths. Passengers who do not conform to the official embarkation arrangements are, therefore, warned that they are liable to forfeit their accommodation if they have not reported to H.M. Immigration Officers by 11.30 a.m. at the latest.

[The document also listed the agents for the New Zealand Shipping Company and the restaurants in the vicinity of St. Enoch Station]

AGENTS

J.B. Westray & Co. Ltd, 138, Leadenhall Street, London E.C.3. Telegrams: Interview, Stock, London. Telephone: AVEnue 5220

P. Henderson & Co. 95 Bothwell Street, Glasgow, G.2. Telegrams: Carthage, Glasgow. Telephone: CENtral 8761

Restaurants in the Vicinity of St Enoch Station, Glasgow

Ca'Doro Restaurant, 122, Union Street, C.1. Breakfast from 7 a.m.

Miss Rombach's Restaurant, 5, Waterloo Street, C.2. Breakfast from 7 a.m.

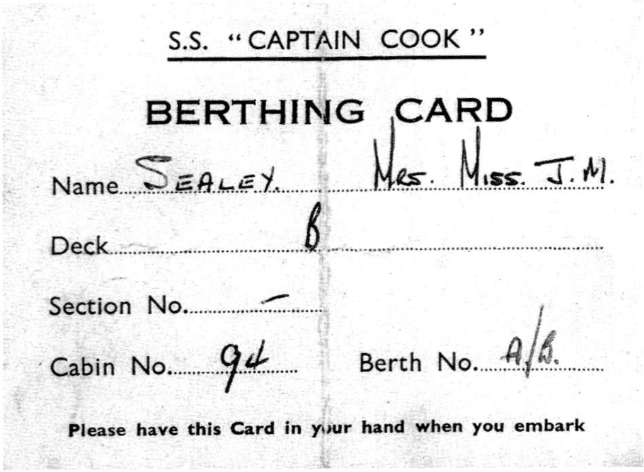
S.S. "CAPTAIN COOK"

BERTHING CARD

Name SEALEY Mrs. Miss. J.M.

Deck B

Section No. —

Cabin No. 94 Berth No. A/B.

Please have this Card in your hand when you embark

Berthing Card for the Sealey family showing their berth as Deck B, Cabin 94, Berth A/B.

[Document 26 March 1954, from The New Zealand Shipping Company, 138 Leadenhall Street, London E.C.3.]

S.S. "CAPTAIN COOK"

Leaves Glasgow	13th April, 1954
Due Curacao	25th April
Due Panama	28th April
Due Wellington	18th May

Latest dates for posting letters by air mail G.P.O. London.

18th April,..... (name)
Passenger "CAPTAIN COOK"
C/- Messrs. S.E.L.Maduro & Sons, Inc.,
Curacao, D.W.I

21st April,..... (name)
Passenger "CAPTAIN COOK"
C/- Messrs. Norton Lilly & Co.
P.O.Box 5017,
Cristobal, Canal Zone.

8th May,..... (name)
Passenger "CAPTAIN COOK"
(Draft 35
(C/- Department of Labour
(P.O.Box 6310
(Wellington, New Zealand

Cables may be sent during the voyage up to the following dates addressed as under:

23rd April,..... (name)
Passenger "CAPTAIN COOK"
Care Maduroship
CURACAO

26th April,..... (name)
Passenger "CAPTAIN COOK"
Care Vernotch
CRISTOBAL

16th May,..... (name)
Passenger "CAPTAIN COOK"
Care Conrad
WELLINGTON

The above address marked applies only to passengers travelling under the New Zealand Migration Scheme. Mails for all Services and Service dependants should be addressed care The New Zealand Shipping Co. Ltd., P.O.Box 1699, Wellington, New Zealand, and the envelope should also show the respective Service Department concerned.

It is essential that all letters bear the PASSENGER'S NAME, as well as the NAME OF THE VESSEL on the envelope as the omission of this information will lead to the non-delivery of your letter.

[Undated document from The Director of Employment, The New Zealand Department of Labour and Employment Immigration Division]

WELCOME TO NEW ZEALAND

Dear New Settlers,

I wish to take this early opportunity of welcoming you upon your arrival in New Zealand under the Government's Immigration Scheme.

In a separate advice you will find particulars of the position to which you have been appointed. Arrangements have been made for you to proceed there as soon as practicable. The officers of this Department who are meeting you at the ship will issue any travel tickets necessary to convey you to your destination.

While I am sure you will quickly make friends with many New Zealanders, you will no doubt find that, in the process of settling in, there will be occasions when you will wish to turn to someone for advice or assistance on many of the matters that confront a stranger arriving in a new country.

Whilst your fellow workers will, I am sure, do all they can to assist you, I would like you to know that this Department is available and anxious to assist or advise you at any time on any matters on which you may require help. If you experience any difficulties, I would ask you to contact the District Office of this Department at the centre to which you are proceeding.

Immigration Welfare Committees have been set up in each of the centres of the Dominion where the Department has District Offices. The Committees are voluntary organizations set up for the purpose of making available to new settlers the services of organizations interested in assisting and advising them, and generally enabling new settlers to be satisfactorily settled in and absorbed into the community. The Committees can arrange contacts with, and introductions to, Church bodies, sports bodies, social clubs, and other forms of organized social activity. Any officer of the Department will advise you how to get in touch with the nearest Immigration Welfare Committee.

I trust you will find your new position interesting and pleasant, and that you will have no occasion to regret the decision you made to come to New Zealand.

[Completed form Imm. 21, undated, from the Director of Employment, Immigration Department, Department of Labour and Employment.]

NEW ZEALAND

DEPARTMENT OF LABOUR AND EMPLOYMENT

IMMIGRATION DEPARTMENT

PARTICULARS OF EMPLOYMENT AND ACCOMMODATION

Name: Mr J.H. SEALEY

Draft No. 35 "CAPTAIN COOK"

You have been appointed to a position as **SHEETMETAL ERECTOR**

with **MODERN SHEETMETALS WORKS LTD** at **120 PARK ROAD, AUCKLAND C.3**

Accommodation arranged: **PRIVATE BOARD**

Disembarkation : You will disembark from the ship at the time stated on your DISEMBARKATION NOTICE. All transport arrangements have been made for you. Officers of the Department will attend to the on-forwarding of your personal heavy luggage. Please ensure that the hand luggage you will be carrying with you is clearly marked with your name and destination.

Contract : Your attention is drawn to the conditions in your Agreement with the New Zealand Government. **You must obtain the prior approval of the nearest District Officer of this Department before you can leave the employer with whom you have been placed.**

Your nearest District Office is at AUCKLAND

Any settler failing to honour the terms of the contract is liable to be required to refund the cost of the steamer fare from the United Kingdom to New Zealand. In addition, married settlers are liable for the fares of their wives and children.

In your own case this would amount to £258. 0. 0 sterling. This advice is given as a matter of form, so that you may be aware of your commitment under the contract.

Mail : Please advise your friends and relatives overseas of your new address as soon as possible after your arrival at your destination.

Director of Employment.

Lab.—Imm. 21]

[40,000/9/52—6555

Form 21 advising John Sealey of the particulars of his employment and accommodation.

PARTICULARS OF EMPLOYMENT AND ACCOMMODATION

Name: Mr J.H. SEALEY

Draft No. 35 "CAPTAIN COOK"

You have been appointed to a position as SHEETMETAL ERECTOR with MODERN SHEETMETALS WORKS LTD at 120 PARK ROAD, AUCKLAND C.3.

Accommodation arranged: PRIVATE BOARD.

Disembarkation: You will disembark from the ship at the time stated on your DISEMBARKATION NOTICE. All transport arrangements have been made for you. Officers of the Department will attend to the on-forwarding of your personal heavy luggage. Please ensure that the hand luggage you will be carrying with you is clearly marked with your name and destination.

Contract: Your attention is drawn to the conditions in your Agreement with the New Zealand Government. You must obtain the prior approval of the nearest District Officer of this Department before you can leave the employer with whom you have been placed.

Your nearest District Office is at AUCKLAND.

Any settler failing to honour the terms of the contract is liable to be required to refund the cost of the steamer fare from the United Kingdom to New Zealand. In addition, married settlers are liable for the fares of their wives and children.

In your own case this would amount to £258.0.0 sterling. This advice is given as a matter of form, so that you may be aware of your commitment under the contract.

Mail: Please advise your friends and relatives overseas of your new address as soon as possible after your arrival at your destination.

Illustrations acknowledgement

All photographs and other original material were supplied by Janet Haines (nee Sealey).

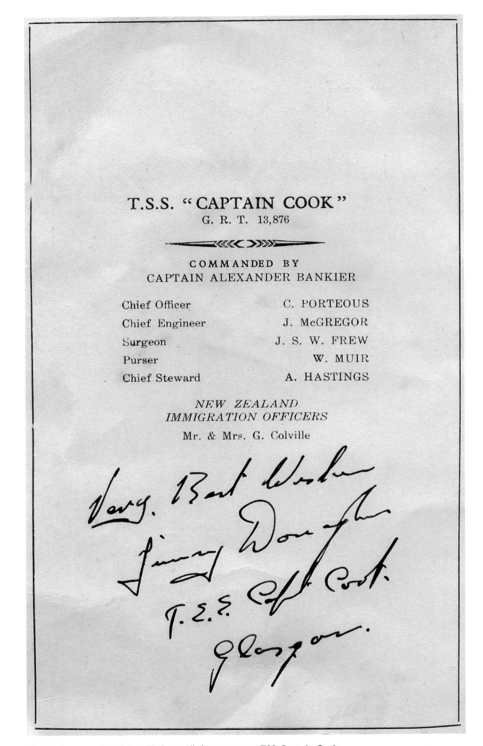

T.S.S. "CAPTAIN COOK"
G. R. T. 13,876

COMMANDED BY
CAPTAIN ALEXANDER BANKIER

Chief Officer	C. PORTEOUS
Chief Engineer	J. McGREGOR
Surgeon	J. S. W. FREW
Purser	W. MUIR
Chief Steward	A. HASTINGS

NEW ZEALAND
IMMIGRATION OFFICERS
Mr. & Mrs. G. Colville

Very. Best Wishes
Jimmy Dougherty
T.S.S. Capt Cook.
Glasgow.

The back page of Cathie Hill's farewell dinner menu, TSS *Captain Cook*.

CHAPTER 16

Pamela Brown

Name	Pamela Mary Brown
Ship	TSS *Captain Cook*
Departure date	25 January 1955
Arrival date	3 March 1955
Destination	South Island
Age	11

My name is Pamela Mary Robb (nee Brown), born 10 July 1943. I came from Coventry England with my father, Thomas Brown (b 1921), my mother, Phyllis Brown (nee Hanson, b 1921), one sister and two brothers. All of us were born in Coventry, England.

My parents left England to give their children a better and healthier life. I had suffered each winter with rheumatism – so bad sometimes that I was unable to walk and had to use a wheel chair or be carried. I had also been in hospital with a collapsed lung. My sister had an abscess on her lung and suffered constantly with abscesses in her ears – she was profoundly deaf and wore a hearing aid – and one of my brothers had also suffered ill health. So I think our health was one of the main reasons they came to New Zealand, away from the bitterly cold winters where we had to be dug out of our home many times when the snow was up and around the door and windows, and we constantly had to trudge to school in Wellingtons, in snow up to our knees. New Zealand had a far better climate and we never experienced this weather again once we left England.

As well as the English climate there was the polluted air to contend with, which came, I assume, from the factories there. There was always a lot of heavy, smelly, dirty smog that hung low in the air and my parents felt this was one of the reasons we had problems with our lungs and health. New Zealand offered warm, clean and much fresher, less polluted air, and certainly better employment prospects. As far as I knew, my parents intended remaining here. My mother never went back to England but my father went back for a visit when he was in his 70s.

My parents never discussed coming to New Zealand with us children. The first I knew about coming to New Zealand was when my school teacher one day got me to stand in front of the class while she showed a picture of green fields and white woolly animals. She asked everyone if they knew what the animals were, and many of them didn't. Then she told the class I was leaving and going to this place far away over the sea and across to "the other side of the world where they have lots of sheep". Of course she discussed what sheep were used for, meat and wool etc, and showed the class the map of where New Zealand was. This was the only thing I knew about New Zealand before coming here. In those days New Zealand did have a lot of sheep. (This has changed over the years to more cattle, I think.) Of course, being a child, I had nothing to do with the official side of the move. I believe the Church to which we belonged, the Salvation Army, sponsored us to come to Invercargill.

We left a lot of family behind. My Dad came from a family of ten and my mother had one sister, so I left behind paternal and maternal grandparents, many aunts and uncles, great aunts and uncles and a lot of cousins.

I was very close to my extended family and I felt devastated and most unhappy about leaving them. I was very close to both lots of grandparents, and spent a lot of time with my maternal grandmother and cousins. I was close to my Dad but I don't ever remember a time when I was close to my mother, so I felt as if almost everyone I loved had been taken away from me and I was very alone and scared. I fretted for a long time. I would dream every night of trying to find my way back to my grandparents and aunties that I was used to visiting. I tried to retain these memories but over the years, sadly, they slipped away.

As well as our own extended family there was our Church family. The night we left Coventry, the Salvation Army Band that my father had been bandmaster of was there to play us off, along with other Church members whom my parents had known for many years. I remember them playing Christmas carols and "God be with you 'till we meet again". The members of our own family along with our Church family waved us off. We were all very sad.

The trip

We travelled to New Zealand on the TSS *Captain Cook*. We left Coventry by train on 24 January 1955, travelling to the Port of Glasgow for sailing on 25 January 1955. We arrived in New Zealand at the beginning of March 1955, so were at sea for a period of almost five weeks.

I am sure the seas the first few days were very rough and choppy because my mother and sister and I were quite seasick and spent time in the ship hospital, our mother more than the rest of us.

We had a cabin for the six of us and I remember my mother saying that it was "very comfortable" and being very pleased that it had two wardrobes.

I remember the first time we were shown to the dining room. All the tables were beautifully set up – mostly round ones like the one we had, but some longer oblong ones – with white tablecloths and serviettes that stood up in a little peak. I thought they looked like little mountains. In the middle of every table was a vase of flowers.

The Forward Dining Saloon of the TSS *Captain Cook*. The saloon had round and long tables, with peaked serviettes and vases of flowers.

Photo courtesy of Phyllis Young

The first morning we went in for breakfast there was a large half grapefruit placed downwards on each plate. It was the first time I had ever had grapefruit, and I didn't know at that stage what they were. We sprinkled sugar all over them. I thought they were sour but we got used to eating them – although I have never eaten them since!

I also remember a lounge or what the English folk then called a "drawing room". We went in there often as it had a piano and Mother was a great pianist and loved to play the piano. We used to listen to other people playing, too, and sometimes there would be a singsong. We love singing and music.

The carpet had a pattern of big flowers, and above the fireplace was a vase of flowers on a shelf. I used to wonder how it stayed there!

There was great excitement when we went through the Panama Canal. Everyone went up on deck to watch. It seemed to me like there was a wall on either side of the ship and I wondered how we would get through it. I think the ship's engines were turned off at some point and as we sat there the canal was filled up with water and the ship went up. We were pulled through with tugs or some machines that went alongside.

I don't remember if we got off the ship at Panama, but we did get off the ship at a place called Curacao. The name of this place has remained with me throughout the years as it was the very first time we, as children, had ever seen black people. We were quite frightened. They seemed friendly though, and although we could not understand their language and what they said to us, they smiled and laughed

Photo courtesy of Phyllis Young

The lounge of the TSS *Captain Cook* showing the vase of flowers above the fireplace whose security Pamela wondered about.

at us and patted us on the head. They were very amused by the little cap one of my brothers wore. I couldn't understand how the palms of their hands could be so white. Their teeth also were very white.

I'm sure it was here that we had a ride on an elephant. Two of the natives were taking people for rides on these elephants. They had a seat on them and when they got down low on the ground we were helped on.

I'm not sure how long we stayed at this place; perhaps just a few hours while the ship stocked up on supplies. I think this was about 16 or 17 days after we first sailed. I know my auntie had a letter from my mother and she said it was posted on 11 February 1955 from the Paquebo Canal Zone. Passengers were told if they wanted mail posted it was to be left in a box and crew members would post it while they were on land.

It was extremely hot at Curacao and we were not used to the heat, so we were quite glad to get back on the ship out of the scorching heat

I don't remember a lot about what we did on board, although I know that games were often organised for the children – because I wasn't at all sporty I didn't like participating in these. I personally did lots of reading, and we played knuckle bones and "Happy Families", a card game that we had. We didn't take a lot of toys but we did have these few games.

When the siren on board sounded we had to run as fast as we could to the deck to have a life jacket drill, to teach us what to do in case of an emergency. We would see how fast we could get our lifejackets on. It was always quite scary when